The Honour and Dishonour of the Crown

The Honour and Dishonour of the Crown

Making Sense of Aboriginal Law in Canada

Jamie D. Dickson

Purich Publishing Ltd.
Box 23032, Market Mall Post Office, Saskatoon, SK, Canada, S7J 5H3
Phone: (306) 373-5311 Fax: (306) 373-5315 Email: purich@sasktel.net
www.purichpublishing.com

Library and Archives Canada Cataloguing in Publication

Dickson, Jamie, 1975–, author
The honour and dishonour of the Crown : making sense of Aboriginal law in Canada / Jamie D. Dickson.

Includes bibliographical references and index.
ISBN 978-1-895830-83-5 (paperback)

1. Native peoples — Legal status, laws, etc. — Canada. 2. Native peoples — Canada — Government relations. I. Title.

KE7709.D53 2015 342.7108›72 C2015-904863-X KF8205.D53 2015

Edited, designed, and typeset by Donald Ward.
Cover design by Jamie Olson, Olson Informatin Design.
Index by Ursula Acton.
Cover image: Jamie D. Dixon.
Printed in Canada by Houghton Boston Printers and Lithographers, Saskatoon.

Purich Publishing gratefully acknowledges the financial support of the Government of Canada. Its book publishing program is also made possible through Creative Saskatchewan's Creative Industries Production Grant Program.

Printed on 100 per cent post-consumer, recycled, ancient-forest-friendly paper.

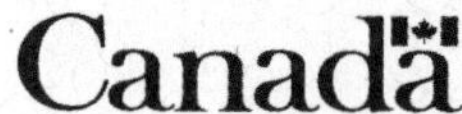

Dedicated to my mother, Sharolyn Dickson

Contents

ACKNOWLEDGEMENTS 8

I: INTRODUCTION 9

II: THE HONOUR OF THE CROWN PRINCIPLE 24
- a. The "honour of the Crown" prior to *Haida Nation* 27
- b. The "honour of the Crown" as reimagined in *Haida Nation* 37
- c. The "honour of the Crown" as applied after *Haida Nation* 44

III: CONVENTIONAL FIDUCIARY LAW 53
- a. Function of fiduciary accountability 61
- b. Content of fiduciary duties 63
- c. Contexts in which fiduciary duties arise 69

IV: FIDUCIARY LAW AS APPLIED, NONCONVENTIONALLY, IN CROWN/ABORIGINAL CONTEXTS 75
- a. Function of Crown/Aboriginal fiduciary accountability 85
- b. Content of Crown/Aboriginal fiduciary duties 86
- c. Contexts in which Crown/Aboriginal fiduciary duties arise 94

V: CROWN/ABORIGINAL FIDUCIARY DOCTRINE AS A "MISTAKE" 103

VI: THE NEW FACE OF ABORIGINAL LAW IN CANADA 114
a. Central role of the honour of the Crown principle 115
b. Limited role for Crown/Aboriginal fiduciary duties 120
i. Conventional Crown/Aboriginal fiduciary accountability 122
ii. Nonconventional Crown/Aboriginal fiduciary accountability 125
c. Practical implications of replacing the "Crown as fiduciary" concept with the "honour of the Crown" principle 132
d. The significance of the mandate to "reconcile" Crown and Aboriginal interests 144

VII: CONCLUSION 148

INDEX 151

INDEX TO CASES 157

ACKNOWLEDGEMENTS

I WISH TO HEARTILY THANK THOSE WHO REVIEWED EARLIER DRAFTS OF this work (or portions thereof) and provided feedback. The list includes: Dwight Newman, Brian Slattery, Sa'ke'j Henderson, Isobel Findlay, Tom Isaac, Rob Flannigan, Ken Cooper-Stephenson, John Whyte, Jonathan Charland, and Rangi Jeerakathil.

I must single out Dwight Newman who supervised my Master of Laws program at the University of Saskatchewan. The thesis I completed as part of that program formed the basis of this book, and I wish to thank Professor Newman for his patience, encouragement, and insight throughout that process. It was a privilege to work closely with such an erudite jurist.

I thank Karen Bolstad and Don Purich at Purich Publishing for their belief that the ideas put forward in this book will make a positive contribution to this complex area of law. It was a pleasure working with them on this project. I also thank Donald Ward, Jamie Olson, and Ursula Acton for, respectively, their expert editing, cover design, and indexing.

I wish to acknowledge Alfred Dawatsare, Gary Merasty, Chief Marie Black and all of my other colleagues and friends at Des Nedhe Development and English River First Nation, including fellow members of the executive team, current Band Council, Elders, trustees, and other band members. It is a privilege and a pleasure to work with you all, and from you all I continually learn.

I would be remiss if I did not thank those many friends and former colleagues with whom I have had insightful discussions about the issues addressed in this book. While I am undoubtedly forgetting some, I thank Liam Mooney, Sean Willy, Derek Rope, Peter Dodson, Trevor McLeod, Jimmy O'Chiese, Brian Kopach, Louise Hahn, Danika Billie Littlechild, Philip Healey, Bonnie Leask, Catherine Twinn, Jerome Slavik, Sam Adkins, Geoff Gishubl, Brian Reilly, Colin Tincknell, Terri-Lee Oleniuk, Dara Hrytzak-Lieffers, Darrel Burnouf, Lisa Ethans, Ryan Leier, Kristin Cuddington, Ellen Quigley, Tim Quigley, and Rob and Shannon Forrester.

Finally, and most importantly, I wish to thank my beautiful wife Anna and our newly-arrived son, Calvin George Allen, for the joy and contentment they bring to my life.

I

INTRODUCTION

> There is a great need for a different kind of legal analysis related to Aboriginal issues which explicitly focuses on Crown obligations. The reciprocal relationship between Aboriginal rights and Crown obligations remains under-theorized and largely unrecognized. This needs to change. . . .
>
> — John Borrows[1]

UNTIL RELATIVELY RECENTLY, CONSTITUTIONAL CROWN OBLIGATIONS OWED to Aboriginal communities were predominantly conceived by the Supreme Court of Canada as being fiduciary in nature, and, to some vague extent, still are. This has always troubled me. One of the disasters of Canada's colonial history is the fact that Crown/Aboriginal relationships have come, more and more, to resemble classic fiduciary relationships — relationships where one party's interests are uniquely at the mercy of the other. I always thought it dangerous to import fiduciary concepts, as the Supreme Court did beginning in 1984 in the *Guerin* decision,[2] to define the legal nature of Crown/Aboriginal relationships. I always felt this development had the effect of reinforcing a paternalistic and constitutionally immoral power structure.

This "Crown as fiduciary" experiment in the Aboriginal context has also just not worked very well, functionally, and by the time the *Haida Nation* case[3] came before the Supreme Court of Canada in 2004, the Su-

1 "Let Obligations Be Done," in Hamar Foster, Jeremy Webber, & Heather Raven (Eds.), *Let Right Be Done: Aboriginal Title, the Calder Case, and the Future of Indigenous Rights* (Vancouver: UBC Press, 2007) at 204–205.

2 *Guerin* v. *The Queen*, [1984] 2 S.C.R. 335, 13 D.L.R. (4th) 321 [cited to S.C.R.].

3 *Haida Nation* v. *British Columbia (Minister of Forests),* [2004] 3 S.C.R. 511,

preme Court had evidently concluded as much. In the Supreme Court's decision in that case, the fundamental conceptualization of Crown obligations in Aboriginal contexts was entirely re-set upon (a) explicitly, the core principle that the Crown is legally mandated to always act honourably in its dealings with Aboriginal peoples, and (b) implicitly, the notion that the regulation of the mischief of Crown dishonour involving Aboriginal peoples is the predominant, if not the exclusive, function of Aboriginal law. The longstanding principle that the Crown is to always act in "a fiduciary capacity" toward Aboriginal peoples was effectively eclipsed in *Haida Nation* by the honour of the Crown principle. In this book, I take a close look at these fundamental, underlying dynamics of Aboriginal law in Canada, revisiting the *Haida Nation* decision and its fall-out some ten years later.

The Supreme Court stated in *Haida Nation* that the honour of the Crown principle may give rise to enforceable off-shoot Crown legal obligations. Three primary types of off-shoot Crown obligation have been explicitly identified to date as flowing from the honour of the Crown principle: (a) the duty to consult and, where indicated, accommodate applicable Aboriginal interests prior to acting in a manner adverse to those interests (conceived in *Haida Nation*),[4] (b) the duty to bring a demonstrably purposive and diligent approach to the fulfillment of constitutional obligations owed applicable Aboriginal peoples (conceived in *Manitoba Métis Federation*),[5] and (c) the fiduciary duty to act "with reference to the best interests" of a First Nation, Inuit, or Métis community in circumstances where the Crown has assumed a sufficient measure of discretion over cognizable legal interests of that community (conceived in *Guerin*, broadened in *Sparrow*,[6] and then fundamentally re-conceived and narrowed through the combination

---

245 D.L.R. (4th) 33 [cited to S.C.R.].

4 This duty was recognized through a trilogy of decisions in 2004 and 2005; *Haida Nation*, *supra* note 3; *Taku River Tlingit First Nation* v. *British Columbia (Project Assessment Director)*, [2004] 3 S.C.R. 550, 36 B.C.L.R. (4th) 370, [cited to S.C.R.]; and *Mikisew Cree First Nation* v. *Canada (Minister of Canadian Heritage)*, [2005] 3 S.C.R. 388, 259 D.L.R. (4th) 610 [cited to S.C.R.]. For recent commentary on this duty, see Dwight G. Newman, *Revisiting the Duty to Consult Aboriginal Peoples* (Saskatoon: Purich, 2014).

5 *Manitoba Métis Federation* v. *Canada (Attorney General)*, 2013 SCC 14, 355 D.L.R. (4th) 577 [cited to S.C.R.].

6 *R.* v. *Sparrow*, [1990] 1 S.C.R. 1075, 70 D.L.R. (4th) 385 [cited to S.C.R.].

of *Wewaykum*[7] and *Haida Nation*). Looked at as a whole, this construct represents the new face of Aboriginal law in Canada.

As will become clear, the Supreme Court would have been better off, in retrospect, by stating explicitly in *Haida Nation* that the newly conceived honour of the Crown principle was developed to entirely eclipse its fiduciary-based predecessor, and to concede the failure of the "Crown as fiduciary" experiment. Put another way, the Court would have been well-advised to fully and explicitly jettison its nonconventional fiduciary concepts from Aboriginal law. I suggest that this is precisely what the Supreme Court has begun to do, in effect, and that it would still be helpful for them to acknowledge as much. The ongoing uncertainty and dysfunction — and the Supreme Court's residual habit of making vague reference to ostensible Crown/Aboriginal fiduciary obligations (we see examples of this in the Supreme Court's recent decisions in *Tsilhqot'in Nation*[8] and *Grassy Narrows*[9]) — is harmful for all involved.

In this book, my primary objective is to conceptualize the emergent fundamentals of Aboriginal law in Canada and, in particular, the Supreme Court's framework for defining Crown obligations owed to Aboriginal peoples. One of my central arguments is that, since Aboriginal and treaty rights were given explicit constitutional standing in 1982, the Supreme Court has not been able to develop a coherent, functional framework in this area. The fundamentals of Aboriginal law are atypically unclear, and this fact is unbecoming our federation. The Indigenous peoples of Canada are entitled to clarity on the types of legal obligations owed them by the Crown. That said, I also argue that developments in recent decisions are helpful and promising.

In order to place my analysis into its proper historical and cross-cultural context, some initial background commentary is necessary. First, prior to the Supreme Court of Canada's decision in *Calder*[10] in 1973, Aboriginal

7 *Wewaykum Indian Band* v. *Canada*, [2002] 4 S.C.R. 245, 220 D.L.R. (4th) 1 [cited to S.C.R.].

8 *Tsilhqot'in Nation* v. *British Columbia*, 2014 SCC 44, [2014] 2 S.C.R. 256 at paras. 80–88 [cited to S.C.R.].

9 *Grassy Narrows First Nation* v. *Ontario (Natural Resources)*, 2014 SCC 48, [2014] 2 S.C.R. 447 at para. 50 [cited to S.C.R.].

10 *Calder et al.* v. *Attorney-General of British Columbia*, [1973] S.C.R. 313, [1973] 4 W.W.R. 1.

groups in Canada were not widely recognized as having independent, enforceable legal rights. The Crown in Canada, likewise, was generally not seen as owing enforceable legal obligations to Aboriginal groups.[11] In *Calder*, however, the Supreme Court held, in an explicit pronouncement of first instance, that Aboriginal peoples do possess collective, independent legal rights. That key finding set in motion events that ultimately led to the enactment of section 35 of our *Constitution Act, 1982* which "recognized and affirmed" the existing Aboriginal and treaty rights held by First Nation, Inuit, and Métis peoples in Canada.

It is a long-accepted principle that rights have corresponding obligations[12] and, accordingly, section 35 may be described as having implicitly enshrined constitutional Crown obligations owed to Aboriginal groups in Canada just as much as it explicitly enshrined Aboriginal and treaty rights. An understanding of the nature of these obligations, however, has been slow to develop after the repatriation of the constitution in 1982. A major reason for this was that there has been substantial uncertainty as to the nature of the rights that were "recognized and affirmed" by section 35. The mechanism that was to provide the critical constitutional fleshing out of the nature of section 35 rights ultimately failed. That is, the oft-forgotten section 37 of the *Constitution Act, 1982* called for a series of constitutional conferences, to take place between 1982 and 1987, wherein section 35 rights were to be fundamentally defined (i.e., it was easy enough to understand what was meant by "treaty rights" cited in section 35, but "Aboriginal rights" was a new term and, essentially, a new and undefined concept).

Unfortunately, the various parties involved in those conferences could not find common ground, the process fatally broke down, and no further constitutional guidance or clarification was presented.[13] It fell primarily to

11 See, e.g., *St. Catharine's Milling and Lumber Co.* v. *The Queen* (1887), [1887] S.C.J. No. 3 (Q.L.), [1887] 13 S.C.R. 577 at 649 [cited to S.C.R.]; and *St. Ann's Island Shooting and Fishing Club Ltd.* v. *The King*, [1950] 2 D.L.R. 225, [1950] S.C.R. 211 at 219.

12 See, e.g., Joseph Raz, *Morality of Freedom* (Chicago: Clarendon Press, 1988) at 166.

13 For commentary on this important period in Canadian history, see generally: James Youngblood Henderson, *First Nations Jurisprudence and Aboriginal Rights: Defining the Just Society* (Saskatoon: University of Saskatchewan Native Law Centre, 2006) at 25–44.

the judicial branch of government, most often the Supreme Court of Canada, to gradually develop legal frameworks for the definition of Aboriginal and treaty rights, which they have done to date through a series of key decisions.[14]

That said, as the nature of section 35-guaranteed "Aboriginal and treaty rights" has been gradually developed by the judiciary since 1982, the nature of corresponding Crown obligations, likewise, has gradually taken some form. This began with the Supreme Court's decision in *Guerin* where a nonconventional form of Crown fiduciary accountability was first conceptualized in an Aboriginal context. Later decisions, prominently *Sparrow* and *Delgamuukw*, further developed a "general guiding principle" for Aboriginal law, mandating that the Crown is always to act in "a fiduciary capacity" in its relationships with Aboriginal and treaty-rights holders[15] which, for the Crown in this context, came to essentially mean acting honourably in their dealings with Aboriginal peoples.[16] Specific fiduciary duties owed by the Crown to Aboriginal peoples were defined in context, and understood as flowing from this general guiding principle.

As I document in Chapter Four, the fundamentals of this nonconventional fiduciary-based construct — developed as the core construct for Aboriginal law in Canada — slowly began to mutate into various, conflicting forms through a series of Supreme Court pronouncements in the 1990s and early 2000s which were often fundamentally inconsistent with one another. Since conventional fiduciary doctrine operates predominantly, if not exclusively, to prohibit conflicts of interest, its application in Crown/Aboriginal contexts had to be stretched well beyond its conventional boundaries, since the Crown so often finds itself in inherent conflicts of interest; its essential role typically involving the balancing and reconciling

---

14 Including: *Simon* v. *The Queen*, [1985] 2 S.C.R. 387, 24 D.L.R. (4th) 390; *R.* v. *Sioui*, [1990] 1 S.C.R., 70 D.L.R. (4th) 427 1025; *Sparrow*, *supra* note 6; *R.* v. *Van der Peet*, [1996] 2 S.C.R. 507, 137 D.L.R. (4th) 289 [cited to S.C.R.]; *Delgamuukw* v. *British Columbia*, [1997] 3 S.C.R. 1010, 153 D.L.R. (4th) 193 [cited to S.C.R.]; *R.* v. *Marshall; R.* v. *Bernard*, [2005] 2 S.C.R. 220, 255 D.L.R. (4th) 1; *R.* v. *Sappier; R.* v. *Gray*, [2006] 2 S.C.R. 686, 274 D.L.R. (4th) 75; *Tsilhqot'in, supra* note 8.

15 *Sparrow, supra* note 6 at 1108.

16 See, e.g., *Delgamuukw, supra* note 14 at para. 190; and *Mitchell* v. *M.N.R.*, [2001] 1 S.C.R. 911, 2001 SCC 33 at para. 9 [cited to S.C.R.].

of interests.[17] It was often acknowledged — explicitly or implicitly — that this nonconventional form of Crown/Aboriginal fiduciary accountability would need to be able to "tolerate conflicts of interest"[18] (i.e., tolerate the very mischief that conventional fiduciary obligations function to prohibit).

In its decision in *Wewaykum*, the Supreme Court effectively commenced a project of mending a materially flawed doctrine. Justice Binnie seemed exasperated in his attempts to explain the implications of the fact that the Crown "can be no ordinary fiduciary" in light of the "many hats" it typically wears.[19] He stressed that not all obligations owed in a fiduciary relationship are themselves fiduciary in nature.[20] However, despite his refrains, Binnie J. still described the content of fiduciary accountability in the circumstances of that case in the same nonconventional manner; still effectively conceptualizing applicable Crown obligations as flowing from a central fiduciary-based principle.[21]

In 2004, and prior to the release of the Supreme Court's decision in *Haida Nation*, Professor Robert Flannigan — a leading commentator on conventional fiduciary law — delivered a searing critique of the Supreme Court's (mis)use of fiduciary doctrine in the Aboriginal context, arguing it was demonstrably, fundamentally based on a "conceptual error," and that the Court's Crown/Aboriginal doctrine essentially involved "a fiduciary analysis in name only."[22]

In *Haida Nation*, though making no reference to Flannigan's critique, the Supreme Court of Canada effectively discarded the nonconventional fiduciary-based principle that had come to be the doctrinal centrepiece of Aboriginal law, though this fact was not explicitly acknowledged in the decision (nor has it been clearly confirmed subsequently[23]). The Supreme

---

17 See, e.g., *Alberta v Elder Advocates of Alberta Society*, 2011 SCC 24, [2011] 2 S.C.R. 261 at para. 44 [*Elder Advocates* cited to S.C.R.].

18 *Mathias* v. *The Queen* (2000), 2001 FCT 480, [2000] F.C.J. No. 1568 (Q.L.) (F.C.T.D.) at para. 473 [*Mathias* cited to FCT].

19 *Wewaykum, supra* note 7 at para. 96

20 *Ibid.* at paras. 83 and 92.

21 *Ibid.* at para. 86.

22 Robert Flannigan, "The Boundaries of Fiduciary Accountability" (2004) 83 Can. B. Rev. 35 at 63 and 65.

23 Note, however, that Justice Deschamps comes close in her minority decision

Court installed a replacement principle to constitute the core of Aboriginal law — the principle that the honour of the Crown must always be upheld in dealings with the holders of Aboriginal and treaty rights — and directed that applicable Crown obligations are to be sourced directly to that principle, and not to an over-arching, nonconventional fiduciary principle.

This book ultimately aims to bring conceptual clarity to this important area of law, the fundamentals of which seem to prove perpetually elusive to lower court judges.[24] In particular, a central objective is to assist the apparent, ongoing process currently being undertaken by the Supreme Court of detangling and extracting the fiduciary-related doctrinal residue from Aboriginal law which, I contend, continues to obstruct the path toward a coherent legal framework.

In undertaking research for this project, I arrived at two unanticipated and remarkable conclusions: (1) the Supreme Court's nonconventional conceptualization of fiduciary concepts in Aboriginal law was later applied by the Supreme Court to other areas of societal interaction with the direct consequence that the very fundamentals of fiduciary law itself shifted and fell into a decades-long process of disrepair, and (2) in three recent decisions outside the Crown/Aboriginal context, the Supreme Court has taken substantial steps toward restoring the conventional fundamentals of fiduciary law which, again, had been unintentionally obscured by the novel developments in Aboriginal law.[25] These conclusions led me to undertake an extensive examination of fiduciary law as part of my effort to isolate the apparent, residual function of fiduciary accountability in Crown/Aboriginal contexts. The results of this examination are illuminating and detailed in Chapter Three.

It is important to note that the experiment by our Supreme Court to

---

in *Beckman* v. *Little Salmon/Carmacks First Nation,* [2010] 3 S.C.R. 103, 326 D.L.R. (4th) 385 at para. 105 [cited to S.C.R.] where she notes that that the honour of the Crown principle has "over time" been "substituted" in for the Crown's fiduciary duty.

24 See, e.g., *Kwakiutl Nation* v. *Canada (Attorney General)* (2006), 152 A.C.W.S. (3d) 552 at para. 26, 2006 BCSC 1368: ". . . aboriginal rights litigation involves lofty, often elusive concepts of law such as the fiduciary duty and honour of the Crown."

25 *K.L.B.* v. *British Columbia,* [2003] 2 S.C.R. 403, 2003 SCC 5 [*KLB* cited to S.C.R.]; *Galambos* v. *Perez,* 2009 SCC 48, [2009] 3 S.C.R. 247 [*Galambos* cited to S.C.R.]; *Elder Advocates, supra* note 17.

construct Aboriginal law on a "Crown as fiduciary" conceptual foundation was literally unprecedented. Inexplicably, no judicial authority was cited in either of the two seminal decisions (i.e., *Guerin* and *Sparrow*) in support of importing fiduciary concepts into the core of Aboriginal law.[26] Likewise, leading academic commentators in this area[27] have largely avoided recourse to conventional fiduciary law in their attempts to conceptualize Crown/Aboriginal fiduciary doctrine, even cautioning against such an endeavour.[28]

Where leading commentators do make reference to conventional fiduciary doctrine, it is perfunctory and disproportionately limited to referencing the decisions of Justice La Forest who, as I will discuss in Chapter Three, was clearly out to fundamentally reconceive conventional fiduciary law in the nonconventional manner conceptualized in the Crown/Aboriginal context. Such commentary almost exclusively — and mistakenly — assumes that the fundamental content of a conventional fiduciary duty is a mandate to act in the best interests of another.

---

26 Rather, Dickson J. cited an instance of academic commentary, Ernest J. Weinrib, "The Fiduciary Obligation" (1975) 25 U.T.L.J. 1, for this purpose. Dickson J. did cite two lower court decisions in support one discreet principle related to fiduciary doctrine (*Guerin, supra* note 2 at 384–385) but none in support of his novel interpretation of the main doctrinal fundamentals.

27 Notable commentary from Aboriginal law specialists on the nature of the Supreme Court's Crown/Aboriginal fiduciary doctrine include: Leonard Rotman, *Parallel Paths: Fiduciary Doctrine and the Crown-Native Relationship in Canada* (Toronto: University of Toronto Press, 1996); Brian Slattery, "First Nations and the Constitution: A Question of Trust" (1992) 71 Can. B. Rev. 261; James Reynolds, "The Spectre of Spectra: The Evolution of the Crown's Fiduciary Obligation to Aboriginal Peoples Since *Delgamuukw*" in Maria Morellato, QC, ed., *Aboriginal Law Since Delgamuukw* (Aurora: Canada Law Book, 2009); Kent McNeil, "The Crown's Fiduciary Obligations in the Era of Aboriginal Self-Government" (2009) 88 Can. B. Rev. 1; and the various chapters in Law Commission of Canada, *In Whom We Trust: A Forum on Fiduciary Relationships* (Toronto: Irwin Law, 2002), particularly at 81-113 and 269-293.

28 See, e.g., Slattery, "First Nations and the Constitution: A Question of Trust," *ibid.* at 275; James (Sa'ke'j) Youngblood Henderson, I.P.C., *Treaty Rights in the Constitution of Canada*, (Toronto: Thomson Carswell, 2007) at 897; and James Sakej Youngblood Henderson, "Commentary" in Law Commission of Canada, *In Whom We Trust: A Forum on Fiduciary Relationships, ibid.* at 90.

There appear at least two possible reasons for the fact that both the Supreme Court and leading commentators have avoided recourse to the conventional fundamentals of fiduciary law when interpreting Crown/Aboriginal fiduciary accountability. The first is that the fundamentals of fiduciary law were somewhat unresolved when the Supreme Court sought to import them into Aboriginal law. This argument has been made elsewhere.[29] The second and more compelling reason is that our constitutional morality post-1982 was evidently such that there was a generally observed need for the development of a legal framework for Crown accountability that would strictly and bluntly restrain the Crown's discretionary powers in instances where Aboriginal or treaty rights infringements were threatened. At least ostensibly, aspects of fiduciary law fit the bill, and the endeavour has then been to configure a novel form of regulation only loosely based on fiduciary concepts.

Regarding the above-noted cautions by leading Aboriginal law commentators against recourse to conventional fiduciary analysis in the Crown/Aboriginal context, I contend that they were likely predicated on what is now an out-dated concern. That is, prior to *Haida Nation*, Aboriginal law was lacking an explicit legal principle upon which to conceptualize Crown obligations that correspond to Aboriginal and treaty rights, and to bind the Crown to a high standard of moral dealing generally. It was primarily to this end, and to fill this gap, that the Supreme Court configured its non-conventional fiduciary-based construct. However, as has been shown, the Supreme Court has now instituted its (re-oriented) honour of the Crown principle into this "core" doctrinal position previously inhabited by its nonconventional fiduciary construct; and the entirety of that "fiduciary" construct that came before it is now redundant and serves only to obscure.

Ignoring, then, what I take to be out-dated cautions, and looking to conventional fiduciary law for direct assistance, it is particularly noteworthy that the Supreme Court recently, for effectively all but the Crown/Aboriginal context, rejected the notion that an obligation to act in the best interests of another is either (a) a fiduciary obligation, or (b) capable of judicial

---

29 See, e.g., Mark L. Stevenson and Albert Peeling, "Probing the Parameters of Canada's Crown-Aboriginal Fiduciary Relationship" in Law Commission of Canada, *In Whom We Trust: A Forum on Fiduciary Relationships*, *supra* note 27 at 22.

enforcement in any event.[30] Of course, a Crown obligation to act in the best interests of applicable Aboriginal communities constitutes the very essence of the Supreme Court's nonconventional Crown/Aboriginal fiduciary doctrine. In contrast, in the prevailing conventional framework, an undertaking to act in the "best interests" of another is now actually one of the three main preconditions in the Supreme Court's test for when conventional fiduciary accountability arises;[31] the fundamental nature of conventional fiduciary accountability itself then is something entirely different, as we will see.

In the recent *Manitoba Métis Federation* case, the majority decision of the Supreme Court of Canada held that a Crown/Aboriginal fiduciary obligation could arise pursuant either to the conventional test or to the nonconventional test articulated in *Haida Nation* (i.e., the latter leading to a Crown fiduciary obligation to act in the "best interests" of an Aboriginal community).[32]

This reasoning brings into stark relief just how dysfunctional Crown/Aboriginal fiduciary jurisprudence remains. Its fundamentals are unsound and incongruent. In one of the two ways in which fiduciary accountability may now arise in the Crown/Aboriginal context, a Crown undertaking to act in the "best interests" of an applicable Aboriginal community is a precondition to there being a fiduciary obligation owed; in the other, acting in the "best interests" of the Aboriginal community is the potential fiduciary obligation itself.

These circular dynamics are detailed and unpacked in much greater detail in Chapters Four, Five, and Six, but these initial observations should make clear that it is no longer appropriate or advisable — to the extent that it ever was — to attempt to conceptualize Crown/Aboriginal fiduciary accountability in a vacuum; recourse to the conventional meaning of fiduciary concepts is relevant and necessary. Furthermore, the nonconventional use of fiduciary concepts in Aboriginal law has arguably been destructive for the fundamentals of both fiduciary law and Aboriginal law, and there are substantial gains to be achieved for both in bringing this failed experiment to an explicit end.

---

30 *KLB, supra* note 25 at paras. 44-46.

31 See, e.g., *Elder Advocates, supra* note 17 at 36.

32 *Manitoba Métis Federation, supra* note 5 at paras. 46-50.

This book is organized around seven chapters. In the next chapter, Chapter Two, I undertake a substantial examination of the modern honour of the Crown principle (i.e., the prevailing conceptual foundation of Aboriginal law in Canada). I begin by mining the historical jurisprudence in order to identify the jurisprudential roots of the "honour of the Crown" concept. I then detail the manner in which the honour of the Crown principle is re-oriented in *Haida Nation*, and I argue that Crown honour accountability in Aboriginal law in Canada now has demonstrable conceptual parameters; its fundamental components have come into view and appear capable of consistent application and development. Finally, I address the applicable, significant Supreme Court developments on the honour of the Crown principle since *Haida Nation* (most notably, the Court's decision in *Manitoba Métis Federation*).

In Chapter Three, I provide a detailed overview of the fundamentals of conventional fiduciary law in Canada in order to help understand the role we may expect it to play in Crown/Aboriginal contexts moving forward. Specifically, I examine three incidents of the doctrine: (1) the function of fiduciary law; (2) the general content of fiduciary accountability (specifically, the nature of fiduciary obligations and fiduciary breaches); and (3) the specific contexts in which fiduciary accountability arises.

Generally, the function of conventional fiduciary law is the protection of beneficiary interests in trust-like contexts against the singular mischief of self-interested conduct by their fiduciary. The content of a conventional fiduciary obligation typically involves a strict and absolute prohibition (absent consent) against putting one's own interests in conflict with those applicable, entrusted interests of a beneficiary. Such conventional fiduciary obligations arise in contexts where one undertakes to act exclusively in regard to the critical interests of another, having assumed or been assigned a specific discretionary power in relation to the management of those interests such that there is vulnerability in the arrangement.[33]

In Chapter Four, I examine the Supreme Court's nonconventional application of fiduciary concepts in the Crown/Aboriginal context. I track the major developments beginning with *Guerin* and then examine the current Supreme Court conceptualization of Crown/Aboriginal fiduciary accountability. Mirroring the structure of Chapter Three, I organize the analysis

33 The most recent articulation by the Supreme Court of the prevailing test is in *Elder Advocates*, *supra* note 17 at para. 36.

around (1) the function of Crown/Aboriginal fiduciary accountability, (2) its content, and (3) the contexts in which it arises. In brief sum, the function is uncertain, seemingly duplicative of the function of Crown honour accountability (i.e., to regulate against dishonourable Crown conduct in Aboriginal contexts). The content of the nonconventional *Haida Nation*-framed Crown/Aboriginal fiduciary obligation involves a prescriptive obligation which, once triggered, mandates the Crown to act with reference to the best interests of an applicable Aboriginal community. The obligation arises when the Crown has assumed a sufficient amount of discretion over specific, cognizable Aboriginal interests. I identify three possible (and distinct) ways to interpret this mandate, and consider the merits of each.

In Chapter Five, I invoke Ronald Dworkin's concept of judicial mistakes and make the case that the Supreme Court's use of fiduciary concepts in Aboriginal law qualifies. The late Ronald Dworkin's "rights thesis" has long been regarded as a preeminent legal theory which has dramatically influenced western understandings of the fundamental nature of law and adjudication in common law systems. Put simply, it is a comprehensive and helpful model for understanding how law, essentially, works.[34]

The Supreme Court in *Guerin* demonstrably misinterpreted the longstanding fundamentals of fiduciary law and erred by applying a novel interpretation without acknowledging it was radically altering the doctrinal fundamentals. I argue that, in accordance with Dworkin's account, the Supreme Court's nonconventional Crown/Aboriginal fiduciary doctrine ought to be entirely disqualified on that basis, and that in *Haida Nation* the Supreme Court effectively but not explicitly acknowledged as much.

In Chapter Six, I comment on what the future appears to hold for Aboriginal law in Canada, bringing to bear on that inquiry the conclusions I draw in earlier chapters. In the first part of Chapter Six, I provide a brief synopsis of the central role that the honour of the Crown principle is configured to play moving forward. As the doctrinal anchor of Aboriginal law

34 Notably, the Supreme Court of Canada, for its part, relied on Dworkin's thesis in several cases in the 1980s where conceptualizing constitutional rights in Canada post-1982. See, e.g., *Attorney General of Quebec* v. *Grondin,* [1983] 2 S.C.R. 364, 4 D.L.R. (4th) 605; *R.* v. *Edwards Books and Art Ltd.*, [1986] 2 S.C.R. 713, [1986] S.C.J. No. 70 (Q.L.); and *R.* v. *Therens*, [1985] 1 S.C.R. 613, [1985] S.C.J. No. 30 (Q.L.). See, also, *Re Residential Tenancies Act*, [1981] 1 SCR 714, 123 D.L.R. (3d) 554; and *R.* v. *Paré*, [1987] 2 SCR 618, 45 D.L.R. (4th) 546.

— as it was described by Justice Binnie in *Little Salmon/Carmacks*[35] — the honour of the Crown principle describes the core mandate of this area of law — that the Crown is to act honourably in its dealings with Aboriginal peoples — and operates to give rise to specific and enforceable obligations, the breach of which by the Crown violates the anchor principle.

In the second part of Chapter Six, I summarize the ongoing applicability of fiduciary duties in Crown/Aboriginal contexts. Following the directive in *Manitoba Métis Federation* that there are now, effectively, two different types of Crown/Aboriginal fiduciary accountability — the conventional and the nonconventional — I examine each in turn. In light of the fact that conventional fiduciary law has been substantially clarified in a recent line of cases, it is now a relatively straightforward exercise to envisage, at a high level of abstraction, how conventional fiduciary accountability will apply in Crown/Aboriginal contexts moving forward. I construct some hypothetical scenarios for illustration purposes.

In contrast, when it comes to conceptualizing the application of (*Wewaykum*, and *Haida Nation*-framed) nonconventional Crown/Aboriginal fiduciary duties, the irresistible conclusion is that (a) there is simply no longer any reason to maintain them as part of this area of law, and (b) maintaining them actually serves to obscure. Ultimately, I propose a jettisoning of this hollow vestige of a flawed and largely discarded framework.

In the third part of Chapter Six, I comment on the practical implications of replacing the nonconventional Crown as fiduciary concept with the honour of the Crown principle. Some may feel as though there is little if anything that turns on the question of whether Aboriginal law is fundamentally predicated on (a) a "Crown as fiduciary" principle that stipulates, effectively, that the Crown must act honourably in its dealings with Aboriginal peoples, or (b) an "honour of the Crown" principle that, of course, stipulates precisely the same thing. To some extent, this shift may be perceived as a simple name change. My contention is that there is much more to it, and that this is a name change with positive, transformative potential.

In addition to commenting on what I see as the positive implications of this change — which are mostly related to the need for clarity on the nature of the obligations owed by the Crown to Aboriginal peoples in Canada — I endeavour to pinpoint the nature of the apparent resistance among some (including, as already noted, the Supreme Court of Canada) to fully

35 *Supra* note 23 at para. 42.

letting go of this idea that Crown/Aboriginal relationships are still somehow fundamentally fiduciary in nature. Unfortunately, pin-pointing the nature of this resistance is no small task. I was not able to locate in either the jurisprudence or in the *post-Haida Nation* academic commentary any notable substantive argument against replacing the vestigial "Crown as fiduciary" concept with the "honour of the Crown" principle (i.e., some have expressed resistance, explicitly or implicitly, without explaining the basis for such resistance). That said, I speculate to some extent, and I confront this resistance by contending that there is nothing substantive to be lost (and much to be gained) in fully and finally releasing the nonconventional Crown as fiduciary concept from Aboriginal law.

In the final part of Chapter Six, I address the significance of the fact that this new Crown honour-based legal framework is often explicitly set against a backdrop of the oft-noted mandate of reconciling the pre-existence of Aboriginal societies, on the one hand, with the reality of assumed Crown sovereignty, on the other. I posit that while the judiciary is responsible, under the new framework, for regulating the mischief of Crown dishonour, it does not play a direct role in effecting the constitutional reconciliation of Crown and Aboriginal interests; rather, it plays an indirect supporting role. The reconciliation project is to be undertaken by the executive and legislative branches of government, working collaboratively with Aboriginal peoples. The judiciary's function in sanctioning specific instances of Crown dishonour (which arguably constitutes the full extent of its role) is meant to protect and facilitate the over-arching reconciliation project. It is helpful to explicitly identify responsibilities in this fashion in order to ensure that the executive and legislative branches of government do not unwittingly (or wittingly) off-load their obligations to the judiciary, the latter having no capacity to discharge the applicable reconciliation undertaking.

Before moving on to Chapter Two, it is noteworthy that at various points in the chapters to follow, I make some use of Dworkinian terminology. As already indicated, I make central use of Dworkin's concept of judicial mistakes in Chapter Five. In addition, I also invoke Dworkin's conception of the related concepts of rules and principles and how each differs fundamentally from the other.[36] Dworkin posits that rules (or duties) operate

36 See, e.g., Ronald Dworkin, *Taking Rights Seriously* (Cambridge: Harvard University Press, 1977) at 24–35.

in all-or-nothing fashion with the effect that if the evidentiary facts a rule stipulates are present, liability necessarily follows. Principles, in contrast, merely incline a decision one way or another, but do not by their form dictate specific results. Rather, principles, according to Dworkin, operate to give rise to specific rights and rules (or duties) in different contexts.

I find Dworkin's account of the operative dynamics of legal doctrine a helpful conceptual tool for the analysis undertaken in this book. Prior to its application in Aboriginal law in Canada, for instance, fiduciary accountability was structured, effectively, as a Dworkinian rule, and not as a principle. The rule took the clear form of a strict prohibition against self-interested conduct in specific factual circumstances. In Aboriginal law, however, it was developed into a confused blend of rule and principle (i.e., the principle taking the form of a fiduciary mandate to act honourably, and specific fiduciary rules/duties understood as stemming from that principle).

I hope that readers (including non-lawyers and non-legal theorists) find my use of Dworkin helpful. I have framed my (fairly limited) use of Dworkin at a high level of abstraction.

II

THE HONOUR OF THE CROWN PRINCIPLE

. . . to know of any injury and to redress it are inseparable in the royal breast . . .

— Lord Blackstone[1]

THE INTRIGUING NOTION THAT CROWN DISHONOUR IN ABORIGINAL CONtexts in Canada may attract consequence was first indicated in early Supreme Court of Canada decisions,[2] though in a historical context, where Aboriginal communities were taken to have no enforceable legal rights, constitutional or otherwise.[3] Years later, that notion was picked up by the Supreme Court in *Sparrow*,[4] and then incrementally expanded and transformed through, principally, *Badger*,[5] *Marshall No. 1*,[6] *and Haida Nation*.

1 William Blackstone, *Commentaries on the Laws of England; in Four Books*, Thomas Cooley, ed., (Chicago: Callaghan and Cockraft, 1871) Book 3, c. 17 at paras. 254–255 [*Blackstone Commentaries*], cited in Thomas Isaac, *Aboriginal Law: Commentary and Analysis* (Saskatoon: Purich, 2012) at 313.

2 *Province of Ontario* v. *Dominion of Canada and Province of Quebec; In re Indian Claims*, [1895] S.C.J. No. 96 (Q.L.), (1895) 25 S.C.R. 434 at 512 [cited to S.C.R.]; *R.* v. *George* (1966), 55 D.L.R. (2d) 386, [1966] S.C.R. 267 [*George* cited to S.C.R.].

3 See, e.g., *St. Catharine's Milling and Lumber Co.* v. *The Queen* (1887), [1887] S.C.J. No. 3 (Q.L.), [1887] 13 S.C.R. 577 at 649 [cited to S.C.R.]; and *St. Ann's Island Shooting and Fishing Club Ltd.* v. *The King*, [1950] 2 D.L.R. 225, [1950] S.C.R. 211 at 219.

4 *R.* v. *Sparrow*, [1990] 1 S.C.R. 1075, 70 D.L.R. (4th) 385 [cited to S.C.R.].

5 *R.* v. *Badger*, [1996] 1 S.C.R. 771, [1996] 2 C.N.L.R. 77 [cited to S.C.R.].

6 *R.* v. *Marshall* (1999), 177 D.L.R. (4th) 513, [1999] 3 S.C.R. 456 [cited to S.C.R.].

While under-theorized, it is now the central organizing principle for Aboriginal law in Canada.[7]

Anecdotally, one jurist appears uniquely responsible for the fact that the honour of the Crown principle now occupies such a core doctrinal position. As Associate Chief Justice of the Ontario Court of Appeal, the late Bert James MacKinnon pronounced in *R.* v. *Taylor and Williams* that "the honour of the Crown is always involved" in the process of treaty interpretation in Canada.[8] This was an argument that he, in his earlier days as a practitioner, had advanced on behalf of his client, Calvin George, in litigation that saw the first twentieth century-invocation by the Supreme Court of Canada of the honour of the Crown principle in an Aboriginal context (and the only such invocation prior to *Sparrow*).[9] MacKinnon A.C.J.O's pronouncement in *Taylor and Williams* was then ultimately adopted in *Sparrow*.[10]

In *Haida Nation*, the honour of the Crown precept was elevated to the status of being the central organizing principle in this area.[11] Where honour may have been judicially invoked previously as explicit acknowledgment of non-binding political or moral-only obligations,[12] Crown dishonour in applicable Aboriginal contexts is now legally actionable in Canada (i.e., through enforcement of the specific off-shoot Crown duties flowing from the honour of the Crown principle). Chief Justice McLachlin's decision in *Haida Nation* also suggests that this new or reconfigured theory of Crown obligation is intended to both reorient previous doctrine in the

---

7 As made very clear in cases like *Beckman* v. *Little Salmon/Carmacks First Nation,* [2010] 3 S.C.R. 103, 326 D.L.R. (4th) [cited to S.C.R.]; and *Manitoba Métis Federation* v. *Canada (Attorney General)*, 2013 SCC 14, 355 D.L.R. (4th) 577 [cited to S.C.R.].

8 [1981] 3 C.N.L.R. 114, 34 O.R. (2d) 360 [cited to C.N.L.R.].

9 *George, supra* note 2 at 102.

10 *Sparrow, supra* note 4 at 1108.

11 *Haida Nation* v. *British Columbia (Minister of Forests),* [2004] 3 S.C.R. 511, 245 D.L.R. (4th) 33 at para. 16–20 [cited to S.C.R.].

12 See, e.g., *Ontario Mining Co. Ltd.* v. *Seybold,* [1903] A.C. 73, (1902) 72 L.J.P.C. 5 at 81 and 82 [cited to A.C.]; and *Province of Ontario* v. *Dominion of Canada,* [1909] S.C.J. No. 28 (Q.L.), [1909] 42 S.C.R. 1 at paras. 209–210 and 217–218 [cited to Q.L.].

area[13] and spawn new doctrinal frameworks.

Unfortunately, however, substantial confusion persists. This confusion appears a manifestation of prevailing uncertainty as to the nature and scope of residual, parallel applicability of Crown/Aboriginal fiduciary accountability. Lower courts have struggled to understand the fundamentals of the doctrine, and, as one leading commentator recently put it in relation to the honour of the Crown principle, "a complete understanding of this important legal principle . . . is in its infancy."[14] Oddly, and with some notable exceptions,[15] there is also a dearth of (post-*Haida Nation*) academic commentary on the honour of the Crown principle, particularly as regards the doctrinal intersection between the honour of the Crown principle and Crown/Aboriginal fiduciary accountability.

It is the prevailing confusion in the lower courts and the lack of applicable academic commentary that inspired this book. Doctrinal clarity in this area is lacking and imperative. In this chapter, I attempt to conceptualize both the historical pedigree of the honour of the Crown principle and its contemporary parameters, as discernible at this early stage in its development.

---

13 As an example, in *Mitchell* v. *M.N.R.*, [2001] 1 S.C.R. 911, 2001 SCC 33 at para. 9 [cited to S.C.R.], the fundamental nature of Crown/Aboriginal fiduciary accountability was referred to by McLachlin C.J. as "an obligation to treat aboriginal peoples fairly and honourably, and to protect them from exploitation, a duty characterized as 'fiduciary.'" However, in *Haida Nation, supra* note 11 at para. 32, where the Chief Justice referenced this passage from *Mitchell* when talking about Crown liability as being Crown honour-based, she left out the final five words of that passage from *Mitchell.*

14 Isaac, *Aboriginal Law, supra* note 1 at 312.

15 See, e.g., Dwight G. Newman, *Revisiting the Duty to Consult Aboriginal Peoples* (Saskatoon: Purich, 2014) at 26–28; Brian Slattery, "Aboriginal Rights and the Honour of the Crown" (2005) 29 S.C.L.R. (2d) 433; Isaac, *Aboriginal Law, supra* note 1 at 312–326; and J. Timothy S. McCabe, *The Honour of the Crown and its Fiduciary Duties to Aboriginal Peoples* (Markham: LexisNexis Canada, 2008) at 67–146; and James (Sa'ke'j) Youngblood Henderson, I.P.C., *Treaty Rights in the Constitution of Canada*, (Toronto: Thomson Carswell, 2007) at 887–944.

a. The "honour of the Crown" prior to *Haida Nation*

Beginning, then, with the historical roots of the honour of the Crown principle, early commentary suggests it arose in Britain as a principal of equity in the context of an imperial constitution premised on broad Crown immunities and largely unfettered Crown prerogatives. The principle, where (seldom) invoked, protected against the Crown inadvertently and unduly exercising its prerogative powers to the detriment of private interests:

> . . . the prerogative of the crown extends not to do any injury; for, being created for the benefit of the people, it cannot be exerted to their prejudice . . . Whenever therefore it happens that, by misinformation, or inadvertence, the crown hath been induced to invade the private rights of any of its subjects, though no action will lie against the sovereign . . . yet the invasion, by informing the king of the true state of the matter in dispute: and, as it presumes that to know of any injury and to redress it are inseparable in the royal breast, it then issues as of course, in the king's own name, his order to his judges to do justice to the party aggrieved.[16]

More recently, in two separate pieces,[17] David Arnot provides a colourful historical account of the practical application of the honour of the Crown principle during times of imperial kingship. On the seriousness with which Crown agents approached the honour mandate, he said this:

> This convention [the honour of the Crown principle] has roots in pre-Norman England, a time when every yeoman swore personal allegiance to the king and anyone who was charged with speaking or acting on behalf of him bore an absolute personal responsibility to lend credit to the king's good name. Should he fail in this responsibil-

---

16 *Blackstone Commentaries*, *supra* note 1 at paras. 254–255, cited in Isaac, *Aboriginal Law*, *supra* note 1 at 313.

17 David M. Arnot "The Honour of the Crown" (1996), 60 Sask. L. Rev. 339; and David Arnot, "The Honour of First Nations — The Honour of the Crown: The Unique Relationship of First Nations with the Crown," in Jennifer Smith and D. Michael Jackson (Eds.), *The Evolving Canadian Crown* (Kingston: McGill-Queen's University Press, 2012) [*The Unique Relationship*].

> ity or cause embarrassment, he was required to answer personally to the king with his life and fortune.[18]

This account betrays a normative ethic of behaviour observed by Crown agents, literally motivated by fear of death, that is unrealistic in a contemporary constitutional democracy such as Canada, despite Arnot's contemporary plea that "[i]n every action and decision the women and men who represent the Crown in Canada should conduct themselves as if their personal honour and family names depended on it."[19] This is not to say that the honour of the Crown principle is inapposite for Canadian Aboriginal law, but rather to say that contextual historical analogy will be of relatively limited value moving forward. The development of the honour of the Crown doctrine in Canada is and will be a novel, contemporary project. That said, and as will become clear, the analysis is incomplete and impoverished without some recourse to the applicable historical jurisprudence.

Tracing the early common law evolution of the honour of the Crown principle is not a particularly arduous task; there are mere handfuls of notable cases prior to *Haida Nation*. That said, there is a discernible evolution. A review of the jurisprudence reveals three distinct threads:

1. The earliest thread, centuries old, involves the invocation of the principle, typically in non-Aboriginal contexts, in scenarios involving contractual and statutory interpretation. It was invoked in such contexts as a shield against technical interpretations that would otherwise ignoble the Crown;
2. The second thread, now over a century old and given its fullest expression in the *Badger* and *Marshall No. 1* courts, involves those cases where the honour of the Crown principle is used as a principle of treaty interpretation in Aboriginal contexts in Canada; and
3. The third, most recent thread, that with which the current project is primarily concerned, includes those cases where the honour of the Crown principle is used to source, and to fundamentally inform, the nature of prescriptive (constitutional) legal obligations owed by the Crown to Aboriginal peoples (i.e., in contrast to the

18 Arnot, *The Unique Relationship*, *ibid.* at 161.

19 *Ibid.* at 162.

proscriptive manner in which it is used in the first two threads).

To the first thread, then, the honour of the Crown as a legal principle goes back at least to the seventeenth century English decisions rendered in *Earl of Rutland's Case*[20] and *The Case of the Churchwardens of St. Saviour in Southwark.*[21] In the latter, it was stated in context that if

> two constructions may be made of the King's grant, then the rule is, when it may receive two constructions, and by force of one construction the grant may accordingly to the rule of law be adjudged good, and by another it shall be adjudged void: then for the King's honour and for the benefit of the subject, such construction shall be made, that the King's charter shall take effect, for it was not the King's intent to make a void grant.[22]

While this early reference to the honour of the Crown principle does not set out a particularly robust legal proposition — i.e., Crown honour requires the avoidance of a technical interpretation that a Crown grant is not actually a Crown grant — there are signs in later jurisprudence under this thread of a general proposition to the effect that the honour of the Crown is to be generally upheld in applicable contractual and statutory interpretations. For instance, the Upper Canada Court of Appeal, in their 1852 decision in *Doe d. Henderson* v. *Westover,* states that applicable incidents of Crown instruments "shall always, for the honour of the Crown be allowed most strongly in favour of the grantee."[23] In a more recent instance, and in an Aboriginal context, the Supreme Court of Canada used the honour of the Crown principle to deliver an equitable interpretation of a tax-related provision of the *Indian Act* that would otherwise have operated to the effect

---

20 (1608), 77 E.R. 555, 8 Co. Rep. 55a.

21 (1613), 77 E.R. 1025, 10 Co. Rep. 66b a 67b [cited to E.R.].

22 *Ibid.* at 1027.

23 (1852), 1 E.&A. 465 (U.C.C.A.) at 468. See also *R.* v. *Belleau,* [1881] S.C.J. No. 28 (Q.L.), (1881), 7 S.C.R. 53 at 71, and *Windsor & Annapolis Railway* v. *R.,* (1885), 10 R.C.S. 335, [1885] 10 S.C.R. 335 at 371. These three cases are cited in Isaac, *Aboriginal Law, supra* note 1 at 312–314.

of an Indian Band being "disposed of . . . [certain statutory] entitlements."[24]

As an aside, it is noteworthy that in certain other instances, the honour of the Crown principle was at times invoked not as a principle of law or equity but more as a judicial acknowledgement of perceived governance ethics. To this end, note that prior to the *Calder* decision in 1973 and the subsequent constitutionalization of Aboriginal and treaty rights in 1982, "rights" held by Aboriginal peoples were commonly regarded as being entirely "dependent on the good will of the sovereign."[25] This notion of the "good will of the Sovereign" as something expected in a political context but non-enforceable at law, closely resembles the honour of the Crown principle as articulated in such early invocations.

One such early invocation is found in the decision in *Ontario Mining Co. Ltd.* v. *Seybold.*[26] This case involved a dispute between two mining companies, each of which wanted to develop portions of surrendered reserve lands. At issue was the effect of the *Indian Act*-based surrender of the lands to Canada by a First Nation. It was held that the surrender implicated the province of Ontario in subsequent ownership and administration. In his decision, Lord Davey of the Judicial Committee of the Privy Council observed that upon the surrender, Ontario "came at least under an honourable engagement" to set aside certain portions of the tract for the use and benefit of the Indians in question (e.g., for hunting and fishing) and that "they could not without plain disregard of justice take advantage of the surrender and refuse to perform the condition attached to it."[27]

The significance of this *dictum* from *Seybold* is that it appears to be the first time in Canadian jurisprudence where there is an instance of Crown honour described as sourcing something close to a positive Crown obligation in an Aboriginal context (unenforceable though the obligation may have been).

Moving to the second thread, the honour of the Crown has become an important principle of equity in the context of Aboriginal treaty interpreta-

24 *Mitchell* v. *Peguis Indian Band* (1990), 71 D.L.R. (4th) 193, [1990] 2 S.C.R. 85 at 133 [cited to S.C.R.].

25 *St. Catherine's Milling, supra* note 3 at 54.

26 [1903] A.C. 73, (1902) 72 L.J.P.C. 5 [*Seybold* cited to A.C.]. See also, *Province of Ontario* v. *Dominion of Canada, supra* note 12 at paras. 209–210 and 217–218.

27 *Seybold, ibid.* at 81 and 82.

tion in Canada. The first jurisprudential indication of an applicable honour mandate in the context of Crown/Aboriginal treaties is found in an 1895 dissenting decision by Gwynne J. In *Province of Ontario* v. *Dominion of Canada and Province of Quebec; In re Indian Claims,* he states:

> the British sovereigns, ever since the acquisition of Canada, have been pleased to adopt the rule or practice of entering into agreements with the Indian nations or tribes . . . the terms and conditions expressed in those instruments as to be performed by or on behalf of the Crown, have always been regarded as involving a trust graciously assumed by the Crown to the fulfilment of which with the Indians the faith and honour of the Crown is pledged, and which trust has always been most faithfully fulfilled as a treaty obligation of the Crown.[28]

More than seventy years after this decision from Gwynne J., the Supreme Court of Canada next invoked the honour of the Crown principle in one of the earliest instances of an Aboriginal litigant seeking judicial protection of treaty rights against the effects of Canadian domestic law. In *R.* v. *George*, Calvin George had been charged and later acquitted in the lower courts of acting in contravention of provincial law by hunting off-season on his Band's reserve lands. At issue was the effect of the Band's treaty hunting rights on the scope of application of the provincial law under which Mr. George was charged, and on the meaning of section 87 of the *Indian Act* of the day (section 88 today) which otherwise made Indians subject to provincial laws of general application. After citing the passage from *Churchwardens*, set out above, Cartwright J. (again in a dissenting judgement, as Mr. George was ultimately unsuccessful) said:

> We should, I think, endeavour to construe the treaty of 1827 and those Acts of Parliament which bear upon the question before us in such manner that the honour of the Sovereign may be upheld and Parliament not made subject to the reproach of having taken away by unilateral action and without consideration the rights solemnly assured to the Indians and their posterity by treaty.[29]

---

28 *Supra* note 26 at 511–12.

29 *George, supra* note 2 at 279.

The use of the honour of the Crown principle here (referenced as "honour of the Sovereign") was in the context, again, of treaty and statutory interpretation, and was invoked toward preventing certain treaty rights from being unilaterally delimited by the Crown.

Interestingly, when the matter in *George* first came before the High Court of Ontario, the Chief Justice of that Court invoked the concept of "a breach of our national honour" in the following statement:

> I wish to make it quite clear that I am not called upon to decide, nor do I decide, whether the Parliament of Canada by legislation specifically applicable to Indians could take away their rights to hunt for food on the Kettle Point Reserve. There is much to support an argument that Parliament does not have such power. There may be cases where such legislation, properly framed, might be considered necessary in the public interest but a very strong case would have to be made out that would not be a breach of our national honour.[30]

The Chief Justice here was arguably implicitly following something like the rationale in *Churchwardens* or *Westover*, but it is nonetheless an interesting early example of a collective concept of honour in an Aboriginal context being invoked in broad terms and in the form of a general restraint on Parliamentary power.

Some fifteen years after *George*, and shortly before the coming into force of the *Constitution Act, 1982*, we see the honour of the Crown principle's next rise, the seminal pronouncement by MacKinnon A.C.J.O. in *Taylor and Williams,* that "[i]n approaching the terms of a treaty . . . the honour of the Crown is always involved and no appearance of sharp dealing should be sanctioned."[31]

This oft-cited passage, as noted above, was first adopted by the Supreme Court of Canada in a non-treaty context (i.e., in *Sparrow*, as discussed in more detail below), and then grounded in *Badger* and *Marshall No. 1* as a key, accepted principle of treaty interpretation. The main applicable passage from *Badger* reads as follows:

> the honour of the Crown is always at stake in its dealings with Indi-

30 *Regina* v. *George,* [1964] 1 O.R. 24, 41 D.L.R. (2d) 31 at (O.H.C.J.) 37.

31 *Taylor and Williams, supra* note 8 at 367.

> an people. Interpretations of treaties and statutory provisions which have an impact upon treaty or aboriginal rights must be approached in a manner which maintains the integrity of the Crown. It is always assumed that the Crown intends to fulfil its promises. No appearance of "sharp dealing" will be sanctioned.[32]

The honour of the Crown principle was invoked in *Badger* as one principle among many informing a larger process of interpreting the scope of a specific treaty right, namely, whether a hunting right extended to include hunting on private lands. General Aboriginal law jurisprudence was, at the time of *Badger*, marked by a growing judicial sensitivity to the need for generous and liberal interpretations of Crown/Aboriginal treaties in Canada[33] against the backdrop of growing recognition of historical injustice in Crown/Aboriginal relationships.[34]

A few years later, in *Marshall No. 1*, Justice Binnie appeared to further elevate the honour of the Crown principle to a more central, doctrinal role in treaty interpretation matters, referring to it repeatedly, and applying it not only to interpret written provisions but to supply perceived deficiencies in the treaty at issue. At the outset of his decision, he said:

> I would allow this appeal because nothing less would uphold the honour and integrity of the Crown in its dealings with the Mi'kmaq people to secure their peace and friendship, as best the content of those treaty promises can now be ascertained. In reaching this conclusion, I recognize that if the present dispute had arisen out of a modern commercial transaction between two parties of relatively equal bargaining power . . . it would have to be concluded that the Mi'kmaq had inadequately protected their interests.[35]

---

32 *Badger, supra* note 5 at para. 41.

33 See, e.g., *Nowegijick* v. *The Queen* (1983), 144 D.L.R. (3d) 193, [1983] 1 S.C.R. 29 at 37.

34 An apt example is a passage from the Supreme Court's decision in *Sparrow, supra* note 4 at 1103, where, using the language of honour, it was stated that "there can be no doubt that over the years the rights of the Indians were often honoured in the breach," and that "we cannot recount with much pride the treatment accorded to the native people of this country."

35 *Marshall No. 1, supra* note 6 at para. 4.

Interestingly, where he reads implied rights into the applicable treaty following earlier Supreme Court precedent (namely *Simon* and *Sundown*[36]), he interprets his mandate to do so, in novel fashion, as flowing principally from the honour of the Crown.[37] This development had the effect of reorienting, to some extent, the conceptual underpinnings of those previous decisions.

I move now to the final thread of *pre-Haida Nation* jurisprudence on the honour of the Crown principle. This third line of case law is distinct from the first two, which saw the principle used in applicable processes of interpreting Crown grants, statutes, and treaties. Here, I track the initial development of the principle as it is ultimately interpreted in *Haida Nation*: as an independent, conceptual source of prescriptive constitutional obligations owed by the Crown to Aboriginal peoples in Canada. The distinction from the first two threads of case law is drawn, partly for conceptual convenience, on the basis that the applicable Crown obligations sourced by the honour of the Crown principle in those threads were in a form that may be described as both proscriptive and largely technical in nature; i.e., obligations not to interpret instruments in a manner ignobling the Crown.

The watershed decision by the Supreme Court of Canada in *Sparrow* is the key decision in this third thread. It was in this decision that the Supreme Court first confirmed that constitutional Aboriginal and treaty rights operate to constrain Crown power generally, and may not be unjustifiably infringed by the Crown. In so doing, they utilized the honour of the Crown principle.

Prior to *Sparrow*, the Supreme Court had determined, in *Guerin*, that in at least some contexts the Crown is legally obligated to act in accordance with a certain (quite undeveloped) high standard of conduct in its dealings with Aboriginal peoples. In *Guerin*, and as I discuss in greater detail in Chapter Four, the dispute involved the manner in which the Crown dealt with Musqueam reserve lands that had been surrendered for a defined purpose in accordance with the *Indian Act*. The Court inaugurated a *sui generis* fiduciary obligation owed the Musqueam (making no reference to the honour of the Crown) but left unclear the scope of that obligation in terms of its future application in Aboriginal law.

In *Sparrow*, another decision involving the Musqueam, the dispute cen-

36 *R.* v. *Sundown* [1999] 1 S.C.R. 393, 170 D.L.R. (4th) 385.

37 *Marshall No. 1*, *supra* note 6.

tred on a claim that the federal Crown had unconstitutionally regulated the Musqueam's Aboriginal fishing rights. While *Sparrow* has vital and numerous implications for various doctrinal components of Aboriginal law, I focus here only on the way in which it interpreted the honour of the Crown principle.

It is axiomatic that wherever there are rights, there are corresponding obligations.[38] In *Sparrow*, the Supreme Court was undertaking, as an endeavour of first instance, to conceptualize the nature of Crown obligations that correspond to the newly constitutionalized Aboriginal and treaty rights. In a crucial passage from the perspective of doctrinal analysis in this area, and after generally acknowledging a history of Crown dishonour in Canada in respect of the treatment of Aboriginal peoples,[39] the Court said:

> In our opinion, *Guerin* [fiduciary obligations], together with *R.* v. *Taylor and Williams* [the honour of the Crown principle] . . . ground a general guiding principle for s.35(1). That is, the Government has the responsibility to act in a fiduciary capacity with respect to aboriginal peoples.[40]

Several observations may be drawn. First, the Court twinned the honour of the Crown principle with the fiduciary mandate to source and forge a central "guiding principle" purporting to restrain and govern Crown conduct in the context of Aboriginal and treaty rights. Second, the standard of conduct contemplated under this directing principle was for the Crown to generally act "in a fiduciary capacity" in its dealings with Aboriginal peoples.

Regarding this second observation, the Court in *Sparrow* subsequently speaks of the importance of "holding the Crown to a high standard of honourable dealing with respect to the aboriginal peoples of Canada as suggested by *Guerin*."[41] Here, since a reference to *Guerin* is clearly a reference to the applicable fiduciary concept, the Court's emerging theory in

38 See, e.g., Joseph Raz, *Morality of Freedom* (Chicago: Clarendon Press, 1988) at 166.

39 *Sparrow, supra* note 4 at 1103.

40 *Ibid.* at 1108.

41 *Ibid.* at 1109.

Sparrow as to the conceptual foundation of Crown obligations in the s.35 context, and certainly that picked up on in later decisions[42] and in academic commentary,[43] is that there was observed to be an over-arching and generalized fiduciary obligation owed by the Crown to Aboriginal peoples, which obligation mandated, as a minimum, the upholding of Crown honour (to some undeveloped high standard).

This conceptualization is consistent with another important passage in *Sparrow* where the Court states:

> we find that the words "recognition and affirmation" [from s.35(1)] incorporate the fiduciary relationship referred to earlier and so import some restraint on the exercise of sovereign power . . . federal power must be reconciled with federal duty . . . [44]

As an aside, and as picked up below, my contention is that this and other applicable portions of the *Sparrow* decision have been meaningfully reoriented; that *Haida Nation* suggests that section 35(1) is now to be read as incorporating the honour of the Crown principle and not the fiduciary relationship.

Moving on, one way to view the outcome and jurisprudential wake of *Sparrow* is that there emerged a competition of sorts between competing principles (i.e., as between fiduciary-based and honour-based accountability) and that while in *Sparrow* the Court explicitly married the two instead of choosing one over the other, it also appeared to stake out an early preference for the fiduciary notion as the emerging, doctrinal centrepiece of Crown liability in Aboriginal law, describing it as effectively absorbing the

---

42 See, e.g., *Delgamuukw* v. *British Columbia*, [1997] 3 S.C.R. 1010, 153 D.L.R. (4th) 193 at 162-168 [cited to S.C.R.]; *R.* v. *Gladstone*, (1996), 137 D.L.R. (4th) 648, [1996] 2 S.C.R. 723 at para. 54 [cited to S.C.R.]; *Haida Nation* v. *British Columbia (Minister of Forests)*, [2002] 2 C.N.L.R. 121, 99 B.C.L.R. (3d) 209 at para. 36 [*Haida Nation BCCA* cited to B.C.L.R.].

43 Rotman, for instance, interpreted *Sparrow* as grounding an obligation applying to "virtually every aspect of relations between the Crown and aboriginal peoples.": see Leonard Rotman, *Parallel Paths: Fiduciary Doctrine and the Crown-Native Relationship in Canada* (Toronto: University of Toronto Press, 1996) at 11.

44 *Sparrow, supra* note 4 at 1109.

honour of the Crown principle.[45] As will be developed in detail in the next section, however, they reverse course in *Haida Nation*.

Subsequent Supreme Court of Canada decisions under this thread interpret *Sparrow* as standing for the proposition that the Crown's *sui generis* fiduciary obligation owed "at large"[46] to Aboriginal peoples in Canada was the over-arching, core principle in Aboriginal law, the obligation to uphold Crown honour arising from that principle. In *Van der Peet*, for instance, Chief Justice Lamer explained that "[t]he Crown has a fiduciary obligation to Aboriginal peoples with the result that in dealings between the government and Aboriginals, the honour of the Crown is at stake."[47]

I move now to examine how the Supreme Court fundamentally re-oriented these dynamics in *Haida Nation*.

b. The "honour of the Crown" as reimagined in *Haida Nation*

The Supreme Court's decision in *Haida Nation* was a seminal decision in Canadian Aboriginal law, following in a thread of other transformative decisions such as *Calder, Guerin, Sparrow, Van der Peet,* and *Delgamuukw*. Installing the "duty to consult and accommodate" as a primary Crown obligation — as the *Haida Nation* decision did together with *Taku River* and *Mikisew* — has entirely transformed the face of litigation in this area.

Consultation and accommodation obligations are now recognized categories of specific Crown accountability in Aboriginal contexts in Canada. In sum, the Crown has a duty to consult Aboriginal communities prior to undertaking or authorizing activity that could adversely impact Aboriginal or treaty rights, and, if the need for accommodation is revealed through consultation, has a companion duty to accommodate the applicable concerns of that community.

Put another way, rights to honourable consultation and (where applicable) accommodation held by Aboriginal peoples are now explicit,

45 As demonstrated in the next chapter, a fiduciary obligation to act honourably toward another is nonconventional.

46 *Guerin* v. *The Queen*, [1984] 2 S.C.R. 335, 13 D.L.R. (4th) 321 [cited to S.C.R.] at 355 *per* Wilson J.

47 *R.* v. *Van der Peet*, [1996] 2 S.C.R. 507, 137 D.L.R. (4th) 289 at para. 24 [cited to S.C.R.]. See, also, e.g., *Mitchell, supra* note 13 at para. 9.

and violation of such rights will constitute actionable Crown dishonour. Frameworks governing the discharge of Crown consultation and accommodation obligations have been substantially animated since *Haida Nation*.[48] However, the development of the conceptual nature of their theoretical underpinnings is a project still in its early stages.

I move now to a detailed examination of the *Haida Nation* litigation, specifically focussed on the manner in which the three respective Courts sourced (or denied) the applicable consultation and accommodation-related obligations claimed. From a theoretical perspective, the decisions are each quite fascinating, and informative for this project generally.

Haida Nation Litigation — Background

For more than a hundred years, the Haida Nation (the "Haida") have claimed title to the lands of Haida Gwaii and the surrounding waters, which claim has not been either adjudicated on its merits or reconciled through any completed process of negotiation with British Columbia or Canada. The Haida lived on these lands long prior to Confederation, were never conquered or displaced, and have never signed a treaty with the Crown.

In 1961, the British Columbia Ministry of Forests granted a permit to MacMillan Bloedel to harvest portions of Haida Gwaii. Over time, the permit was replaced, and later transferred to Weyerhaeuser (in 2000). The latter transfer (as well as some of the preceding replacements) was made after and in the face of express objections advanced by the Haida.

The Haida brought a judicial-review petition seeking, among other claims for relief, a declaration that British Columbia stood in a fiduciary relationship with the Haida and was therefore obligated to consult regarding applicable Haida interests with an intention of seriously addressing those interests prior to making any decisions regarding the management of the timber resources on Haida Gwaii. The Haida also argued that the honour of the Crown was brought into question by the provincial Crown's failure to meaningfully consult.

For its part, the provincial Crown emphasized the fact it had a responsibility to manage the timber resource for the welfare of all citizens of British Columbia, and that it should not be rendered impotent pending for-

48 See, generally, Newman, *Revisiting the Duty to Consult Aboriginal Peoples*, *supra* note 15.

mal reconciliation of Aboriginal rights claims. It argued that no fiduciary obligation could arise in these types of scenarios absent proven Aboriginal rights.

The Haida Aboriginal title assertion is a claimed section 35 right, one that was essentially (assuming eventual formalization) recognized and affirmed by the supreme law of Canada, the *Constitution Act, 1982*. The trial judge noted a "reasonable probability" that the Haida would eventually prove its claim at law.[49]

The *Haida Nation* litigation, therefore, tasked the trial judge, and the appellate courts to follow, with determining the nature of certain consultation and accommodation-related rights against a backdrop of claimed constitutional rights that arguably (though not inevitably) already existed but had yet to be formally accepted or defined.

British Columbia Supreme Court

The trial judge in *Haida Nation* dismissed the judicial-review petition, denying the assertion that the claimed consultation obligations exist at law in scenarios where these types of section 35 rights have been asserted but not yet established or codified (such scenarios are often referred to as pre-proof claim scenarios). Engaging the paradigm of the *Sparrow* justification test (which, as indicated above, provides that infringements of Aboriginal rights may be justified in certain circumstances), Halfyard J. held that since the claimed Haida right to Aboriginal title had not been conclusively determined, and since "the law does not presume the existence of Aboriginal rights,"[50] questions of infringement of such rights were speculative and, as a result, questions of applicable justification (and of the scope of the applicable fiduciary duty or any duty to consult) could not be framed or determined with any certainty.

Despite his acknowledgement that British Columbia owed a generic fiduciary obligation (in some form) to the Haida,[51] Halfyard J. drew a sharp distinction between the nature of moral and legal obligations, and ultim-

---

49 *Haida Nation* v. *British Columbia (Minister of Forests)*, [2001] 2 C.N.L.R. 83 at para. 47, 2000 BCSC 1280 [*Haida Nation BCSC* cited to C.N.L.R.].

50 *Ibid.* at para. 17.

51 *Ibid.* at para. 23.

ately held that British Columbia, in the circumstances of the case, had come under a moral but not a legal obligation to assess the strength of the Haida claim, and to consult proportionately, prior to granting applicable regulatory approvals. He cited, as apparent authority for his distinction between moral and legal duties, the *dictum* of Lamer C.J. from *Delgamuukw,* that the Crown likely has a "moral, if not a legal, duty" to negotiate Aboriginal land claims in good faith.[52]

In support of his finding that British Columbia owed a duty (though moral only) to consult the Haida, he noted the relative strength of the Haida claim to Aboriginal title, the "reasonable probability" that the claim would eventually be successful, and the fact that the claim therefore goes "far beyond" mere assertion.[53] He also cited portions of applicable governmental (British Columbia) consultation policies, which mandated some measure of consultation of Aboriginal interests in pre-proof claim situations, and noted it was "arguable that the Crown . . . failed to comply with its own guidelines, in refusing to consult with the Haida."[54]

It is unclear what purpose he intended his articulation of the existing moral duties to serve, in light of his ultimate finding that such duties are not enforceable at law. The answer to this question may have something to do with his treatment of the honour of the Crown principle, to which end he states that,

> although I have expressed the opinion that the Crown has a moral duty to consult with the Haida concerning the Minister's decision to replace T.F.L. 39, I am not satisfied that the honour of the Crown has been diminished by the past failure to fulfill such moral duty. But I think the honour of the Crown will be called into question if this failure continues.[55]

He appears to have been awkwardly suggesting that moral transgressions of the kind addressed are relevant, for they may in a future instance reach some threshold so as to, somehow in combination with the application of

52 *Ibid.* at para. 61.

53 *Ibid.* at para. 50.

54 *Ibid.* at para. 58.

55 *Ibid.* at para. 64.

the honour of the Crown principle, morph into a type of legally enforceable transgression.

British Columbia Court of Appeal

On appeal, Justice Lambert reversed the decision of Halfyard J. and held that there is a legal duty to consult Aboriginal interests in the pre-proof claim context. Like Halfyard J., Lambert J.A. recognized the existence of an at-large fiduciary relationship between the federal and provincial Crowns on the one hand, and all Aboriginal peoples in Canada on the other. He described it as a trust-like relationship, sourcing back to the *Royal Proclamation, 1763,*[56] that "is now usually expressed" in Canadian courts as fiduciary in nature,[57] and he held that the duty to consult flows from this fiduciary relationship and is itself fiduciary in nature.[58]

He looked at the authorities in relation, principally, to the nature of the fiduciary relationship and then determined that the legal duty to consult is justified by the fact that it would offend the general guiding principle set out in *Sparrow* to deny the legal consultation duty in these circumstances. Specifically, he said:

> the trust-like relationship and its concomitant fiduciary duty permeates the whole relationship between the Crown . . . and the aboriginal peoples. . . . One manifestation of the fiduciary duty of the Crown to the aboriginal peoples is that it grounds a general guiding principle for s. 35(1) of the *Constitution Act, 1982*. . . . It would be contrary to that guiding principle to interpret s. 35(1) . . . as if it required that before an aboriginal right could be recognized and affirmed, it first had to be [established in court]. That is not what s. 35(1) says and it would be contrary to the guiding principles of s. 35(1), as set out in *R.* v. *Sparrow*, to give it that interpretation.[59]

56 R.S.C. 1985, App. II, No.1.

57 *Haida Nation BCCA, supra* note 42 at para. 34.

58 *Haida Nation* v. *British Columbia (Minister of Forests)*, 2002 BCCA 462, 216 D.L.R. (4th) 1 at para. 63 [*Haida BCCA No. 2*].

59 *Haida Nation BCCA, supra* note 42 at paras. 34–37.

Lambert J.A. also commented on the finding of the trial judge that there were only moral duties owed in this instance. He disputed both the reasoning that Lamer C.J.'s *dictum* from *Delgamuukw* supported such a finding, as well as the relevance in any event of the concept of a moral duty to these proceedings.[60]

Lambert J.A. did not specifically invoke the honour of the Crown principle.

Supreme Court of Canada

Chief Justice McLachlin, for a unanimous Supreme Court of Canada, upheld Lambert J.A.'s ruling that there is a legal duty to consult in pre-proof claim scenarios. However, she described the foundation of the duty in much different terms. Following intervening precedent,[61] she adopted a position contrary to both the trial judge and Lambert J.A. on the issue of whether a fiduciary duty is owed at large by the Crown to all Aboriginal peoples in Canada, stating that this duty arises only in relation to "sufficiently specific" interests, and does not exist at large.[62]

McLachlin C.J. held that the legal duty to consult and accommodate exists as progeny of the "core precept" that the honour of the Crown is always at stake in its dealings with Aboriginal peoples. She sourced this underlying honour of the Crown precept in two ways: (1) as a practical result of the assertion of sovereignty by the British Crown over the Haida lands[63] and (2) as a corollary of section 35 of the *Constitution Act, 1982.*[64]

She explained that section 35 constitutes a "promise of rights recognition," describing Aboriginal rights as "potential rights," and stating that during the ongoing process of determining Aboriginal and treaty rights, the Crown must honourably respect the interests that inhere in

60 *Ibid.* at para. 23.

61 The Supreme Court of Canada's decision in *Wewaykum Indian Band* v. *Canada* [2002] 4 S.C.R. 245, 220 D.L.R. (4th) 1 [cited to S.C.R.] was released after the British Columbia Court of Appeal issued its decision in *Haida Nation BCCA, supra* note 42.

62 *Haida Nation, supra* note 11 at para. 18.

63 *Ibid.* at para. 32.

64 *Ibid.* at para. 20.

such potential rights.[65]

Of particular relevance to the current project, she described the doctrinal intersection between Crown honour accountability and Crown fiduciary accountability:

> The honour of the Crown is always at stake in its dealings with Aboriginal peoples. . . . It is not a mere incantation, but rather a core precept that finds its application in concrete practices. . . . The honour of the Crown gives rise to different duties in different circumstances. Where the Crown has assumed discretionary control over specific Aboriginal interests, the honour of the Crown gives rise to a fiduciary duty. . . . [66]

McLachlin C.J. describes the nexus between Crown honour and fiduciary accountability here (i.e., that the former gives rise to the latter) in a manner that fundamentally reverses earlier doctrine. The Chief Justice herself had in *Mitchell* referred to the Crown honour mandate as "a duty characterized as fiduciary."[67] Likewise, recall that Lamer C.J. stated in *Van der Peet* that "[t]he Crown has a fiduciary obligation to Aboriginal peoples with the result that in dealings between the government and Aboriginals, the honour of the Crown is at stake."[68]

Furthermore, though she reconceptualises the honour of the Crown principle as the broader or over-arching source of obligation — the fiduciary duty an off-shoot of this broader constitutional source — she unfortunately does so without acknowledging that fundamental doctrinal reorientation was at play, and that structural conceptual components of previous doctrine were effectively discarded.

On the general content of the honour of the Crown principle, and in contrast to any applicable off-shoot fiduciary obligation which she describes as involving a mandate to act "with reference to the Aboriginal group's best interests,"[69] McLachlin C.J. explains that,

65 *Ibid.* at paras. 20 and 67.

66 *Ibid.* at para. 18.

67 *Mitchell, supra* note 13 at para. 9.

68 *Van der Peet, supra* note 47 at para. 24.

69 *Haida Nation, supra* note 11 at para. 18.

> [p]ending settlement, the Crown is bound by its honour to balance societal and Aboriginal interests in making decisions that may affect Aboriginal claims. The Crown may be required to make decisions in the face of disagreement as to the adequacy of its response to Aboriginal concerns. Balance and compromise will then be necessary.[70]

As will be discussed in the next chapter, notions of balancing the interests of one's beneficiary against those of others and having discretion to compromise a beneficiary's interests in any manner run counter to the very core of conventional fiduciary law that purports to guard against precisely such behaviour. Accordingly, it is unsurprising that the Supreme Court of Canada finally began, in *Haida Nation*, to jettison nonconventional fiduciary concepts from this area of law.

c. The "honour of the Crown" as applied after *Haida Nation*

In the wake of *Haida Nation*'s transformation of the fundamentals of Aboriginal law, lower courts have been at substantial pains to properly conceptualize the prevailing construct.[71] In their defence, the Supreme Court's transformation of its doctrine is not yet complete; the Supreme Court is incrementally mending a materially flawed and dysfunctional doctrine whose fundamentals remain incongruent, and are working to re-orient years of jurisprudence under a new construct. The Supreme Court has not jettisoned the nonconventional fiduciary concepts entirely, leaving significant uncertainty and overlap. Put simply, it is difficult to conceptualize a meaningful distinction between a duty to act honourably toward another and a duty to act with some well-intentioned reference to another's best interest — and hence the confusion in the lower courts.

That said, there have been some notable post-*Haida Nation* developments regarding the doctrinal fundamentals of the Supreme Court's modern honour of the Crown principle. The majority of the jurisprudence

70 *Ibid.* at para. 45.

71 For two representative examples (among many), see *Kwakiutl Nation* v. *Canada (Attorney General)* (2006), 152 A.C.W.S. (3d) 552, 2006 BCSC 1368 at para. 26; and *Callihoo* v. *Canada (Minister of Indian Affairs and Northern Development)*, 2006 ABQB 1, [2006] 6 W.W.R. 660 at para. 77.

in Aboriginal law since *Haida Nation* has been centrally focussed on the honour of the Crown's off-shoot duty to consult and accommodate. The legal framework governing that important duty, and how it applies in both treaty and non-treaty contexts, has been animated substantially.[72] As already indicated, this specific Crown obligation has been, by far, the most litigated in Aboriginal law in recent years.

Comparatively little guidance or clarification, however, has been provided in decisions on the fundamental nature of the honour of the Crown principle itself (and its conceptual nexus with Crown fiduciary obligations). The most significant addition to the law in this latter regard came in the Supreme Court of Canada's recent decision in *Manitoba Métis Federation*.[73] In that decision, the Supreme Court developed what is effectively the second explicit progeny of the honour of the Crown principle, a generic Crown duty to purposively and diligently fulfill applicable constitutional obligations. The nature of that specific duty is discussed shortly. First, I will comment on some of the general clarifications that the Supreme Court has made post-*Haida Nation* regarding its modern honour of the Crown principle.

One of the major themes emanating from the post-*Haida Nation* decisions in this area is the confirmation of the centrality of the honour of the Crown principle in Aboriginal law, and the usurpation by this principle of the jurisdiction previously occupied by the Supreme Court's generalized fiduciary principle. In *Little Salmon/Carmacks*, for instance, Justice Binnie describes the new construct (i.e., the honour of the Crown and its applicable off-shoot Crown obligations) as, effectively, the "essential legal framework" for conceptualizing Crown obligations in Aboriginal law. He describes the honour of the Crown concept as a "constitutional principle," and as an "important anchor" for this area of the law.[74]

Interestingly, in a minority decision in *Little Salmon/Carmacks*, Deschamps J. acknowledges that the honour of the Crown principle has effectively begun to replace the Supreme Court's previous fiduciary-based construct. This is the first instance of the Supreme Court explicitly conceding the doctrinal transformation that has been occurring. In doing so,

72 See, generally, Newman, *Revisiting the Duty to Consult Aboriginal Peoples, supra* note 15.

73 *Supra* note 7.

74 *Little Salmon/Carmacks, supra* note 7 at para. 42.

Deschamps J. also implicitly endorses this transformation on the basis that the previous construct was both paternalistic and doctrinally limited:

> This Court has, over time, substituted the principle of the honour of the Crown for a concept — the fiduciary duty — that, in addition to being limited to certain types of relations that did not always concern the constitutional rights of Aboriginal peoples, had paternalistic overtones. . . . [75]

Additionally, and still speaking in relation to the centrality of the honour of the Crown principle, several other Supreme Court decisions since *Haida Nation* provide statements confirming the transformed and honour-based construct as the new core of Aboriginal law, each in slightly differing but effectively similar conceptualizations.[76]

Another notable and explicit clarification provided by the Supreme Court regarding the honour of the Crown principle is that it is not, by itself, an independent cause of action.[77] Rather, it operates to give rise to enforceable obligations and rights.

Some other notable findings made by the Supreme Court *post-Haida Nation* relating to the nature of the honour of the Crown principle are: that it sources back to the *Royal Proclamation (1763)*;[78] that it applies in the context of modern treaties as well as historical treaties (operating both in an interpretive role[79] and in the context of supplying deficiencies to a written modern treaty[80]); that it may not be contracted out of;[81] that it will

---

75 *Ibid.* at para. 105.

76 See, e.g., *Taku River Tlingit First Nation* v. *British Columbia (Project Assessment Director)*, [2004] 3 S.C.R. 550, 36 B.C.L.R. (4th) 370 at paras. 24–25 [cited to S.C.R.]; *Mikisew Cree First Nation* v. *Canada (Minister of Canadian Heritage)*, [2005] 3 S.C.R. 388, 259 D.L.R. (4th) 610 at para. 51 [cited to S.C.R.]; and *Quebec (Attorney General)* v. *Moses*, [2010] 1 S.C.R. 557, [2010] 1 R.C.S. 557 at para. 116 [*Moses* cited to S.C.R.].

77 *Manitoba Métis Federation, supra* note 7 at para. 73.

78 *Mikisew, supra* note 76 at para. 50.

79 *Moses, supra* note 76 at para. 118.

80 *Little Salmon/Carmacks, supra* note 7.

81 *Ibid.*

at times compel a relaxing of procedural defences that may otherwise be available to litigants;[82] that specific rights that correspond to the duties flowing from the honour of the Crown principle (e.g., the right to be consulted, where applicable) are likely not themselves section 35 rights but rather play "a supporting role";[83] and that despite the various rhetorical pronouncements in multiple Supreme Court decisions that the honour of the Crown is always at stake when Crown representatives are dealing with Aboriginal peoples, it is only actually engaged in the context of constitutional matters.[84]

Manitoba Métis Federation

Manitoba Métis Federation is the first case post-*Haida Nation* where the Supreme Court meaningfully addresses the fundamental, conceptual nexus between Crown honour accountability and Crown fiduciary accountability in Aboriginal contexts. It is also the first instance post-*Haida Nation* where the Supreme Court uses the honour of the Crown principle to conceive a specific type of enforceable Crown honour — that is, a specific off-shoot-type obligation owed by the Crown to Aboriginal peoples. This new obligation — the duty to purposively and diligently discharge constitutional obligations — is the second main Crown-honour-off-shoot varietal conceived by the Supreme Court (*Haida Nation*'s duty to consult and accommodate being the first).

Manitoba Métis Federation involved allegations of Crown misconduct in relation to the carrying out of statutory obligations that had been undertaken by the Crown in the *Manitoba Act* (which is a constitutional document; it is identified as part of the Constitution of Canada in section 52 of the *Constitution Act, 1982,* and appended as a separate schedule thereto). In the complex circumstances in which the Manitoba region was ultimately settled as part of Canada, Métis peoples of the region (specifically a group of French-speaking Roman Catholic Métis, the dominant demographic group in the region) had agreed to become part of Canada after a series of discussions with the Crown. As part of those discussions, the Crown

82 See, e.g., *Manitoba Métis Federation, supra* note 7 at paras. 136–144.

83 *Little Salmon/Carmacks, supra* note 7 at para. 44.

84 *Manitoba Métis Federation, supra* note 7 at para. 66.

undertook a number of specific commitments, which commitments were ultimately formalized as part of the *Manitoba Act*.

Among those commitments was an agreement by the federal government to grant 1.4 million acres of land to eligible Métis children, thus giving them a head start in the context of what promised to be a dramatic influx of non-Aboriginal settlers looking to acquire land. The central issue in the case was whether the Crown was liable for misconduct based on the manner in which it discharged this commitment. Among other problems, the administration of the land grants to Métis children was slow and ineffectual. The main two potential bases of Crown liability considered by the Supreme Court were (1) a breach of Crown honour accountability, and (2) a breach of Crown fiduciary accountability.

Ultimately, the Court issued a constitutional declaration to the effect that the Crown had failed to act diligently in the context of administering the land grants that were to go to Métis children. No other remedy was ordered; the Manitoba Métis Federation had been principally interested in obtaining this declaration which it then planned to utilize as leverage in subsequent negotiations with the Crown.

The case had been largely framed and argued in the lower courts as an alleged breach of Crown fiduciary accountability. However, the Supreme Court determined that fiduciary obligations did not arise in the circumstances of this case. The Supreme Court held that the claimed declaratory relief could be granted on the basis of there having been a demonstrable breach of an enforceable obligation flowing from the honour of the Crown principle. The obligation recognized in the majority decision as having been breached was articulated as a duty to purposively and diligently discharge constitutional obligations that are owed specifically to Aboriginal peoples.

I comment more in Chapter Four on the specifics regarding the manner in which the Supreme Court disposed of the claim of Crown fiduciary accountability. For present purposes, it is sufficient to note that (1) the claim to the effect that the Crown had breached the *Haida Nation*-framed off-shoot fiduciary obligation was denied on the basis that there was no evidence the Métis had a constitutionally protected, proprietary land interest over which the Crown had assumed discretion, and that it therefore did not meet the applicable test set out in the *Wewaykum* and *Haida Nation* decisions,[85] and (2) where the Court also (interestingly) applied conventional fiduciary law to the circumstances of the case, it was explained that conventional fiduciary accountability did not arise in the circumstances of this case because there was no evidence that the Crown had undertaken to act exclusively in the interest of the Métis, which is a precondition to the grounding of fiduciary accountability in the conventional context.[86]

In the majority decision, the facts of the case were found to engage the honour of the Crown principle because, although no section 35 rights were at issue, the explicit obligation owed in this case (i.e., to administer land grants to Métis children) was constitutional and owed exclusively to a Métis collective, and therefore, materially, was linked to the broader Crown/Aboriginal, constitutional reconciliation mandate.[87] Specifically, the majority stated that the *Constitution Act, 1982*, generally, "is at the root of the honour of the Crown, and an explicit obligation to an Aboriginal group placed therein engages the honour of the Crown at its core."[88]

Regarding the specific off-shoot obligation recognized in this case as flowing from the honour of the Crown principle (i.e., the duty to purposively and diligently fulfill constitutional obligations), the majority stated that this duty "varies with the situation in which it is engaged," and that "what constitutes honourable conduct" in any given situation will also vary depending on context.[89] It was stated that the key question, in circumstances where this duty is engaged, is whether or not the Crown acted "with diligence to pursue the fulfillment of the purposes of the obligation," and "in a way that would achieve its objectives."[90]

There are, of course, outstanding questions regarding the scope of this new Crown duty. For instance, the Supreme Court will need to clarify what types of constitutional obligations trigger the duty. As just one example, it is certainly conceivable that Crown obligations undertaken in historical

85 *Ibid.* at paras. 51–59.

86 *Ibid.* at paras. 60–63.

87 *Ibid.* at paras. 68–72.

88 *Ibid.* at para. 70.

89 *Ibid.* at para. 74.

90 *Ibid.* at paras. 83 and 97.

treaties (and perhaps also in modern treaties[91]) will suffice to trigger this form of duty, thus potentially opening the door to an interesting new line of case law in this area. Put another way, this new form of duty gives Aboriginal litigants a new mechanism — mindful of potential limitation period concerns — for use in attempts to hold the Crown accountable for discharging Crown obligations that correspond wih the rights of First Nations set out in treaties; specifically, a new cause of action for instances where the Crown has not diligently or purposively discharged treaty obligations in a manner that upholds Crown honour.

Moreover, as is the case with any newly minted obligation in common law, we can assume the content of this new form of duty will be fleshed out through future decisions, and that the outstanding questions will be addressed. Notably, however, Justice Rothstein wrote a dissent in *Manitoba Métis Federation* that was particularly critical of the majority decision. He described the majority's incubation of the novel Crown honour-based duty here as constituting a dramatic change in the law, not justifiable in these circumstances on the basis that the case had not been framed or argued in the context of that specific duty, and thus that the fundamentals of the duty had not been effectively vetted though the conventional litigation process.[92]

Rothstein J. was also critical of the merits of the duty itself. He was particularly concerned with the lack of a clear framework for determining the specific types of constitutional obligations that would trigger the duty. And he cautioned that recognition of this duty brought with it the "potential to expand Crown liability in unpredictable ways."[93]

For present purposes, the manner in which Rothstein J. conceptualized this new duty in contrast to Crown fiduciary accountability was particularly interesting. He was of the opinion that denial of Crown fiduciary accountability in these specific circumstances ought to have ended the matter. He warned that recognizing the type of Crown honour-based duty that the majority decision articulated "risks making claims under the honour

91 Though the Supreme Court has made comments of late to the effect that they intend to treat modern treaties differently than historical treaties, that the courts ought to "strive to respect [the] handiwork" of modern treaty parties who are more likely to have been "adequately resourced and professionally represented": see *Little Salmon/Carmacks, supra* note 7 at para. 54.

92 *Manitoba Métis Federation, supra* note 7 at para. 204.

93 *Ibid.* at para. 161.

of the Crown into 'fiduciary duty-light.'"[94] He referred to it as a "watered down cause of action [that] would permit a claimant who is unable to prove a specific Aboriginal interest to ground a fiduciary duty, to still be able to seek relief so long as the promise was made to an Aboriginal group."[95] He stated that the new duty has "a broader scope of application and a lower threshold for breach" than would an applicable Crown fiduciary obligation, and he noted that the new duty constitutes a "significant expansion of Crown liability."[96]

Rothstein J.'s reasoning here suggests he was either misconceptualizing the fundamentals of the new "essential legal framework" for Aboriginal law set out in *Haida Nation*, or resisting them. The framework set out in *Haida Nation* is clear that Crown honour-based duties are triggered in applicable circumstances where the impugned facts are not sufficient so as to give rise to Crown fiduciary accountability. That was precisely the outcome in *Haida Nation*: Crown fiduciary accountability was denied on the basis that the Aboriginal interest was insufficiently specific (i.e., since the Aboriginal right in question was asserted but not yet established or codified). Yet, a Crown honour-based obligation — the duty to consult and accommodate — was recognized and enforced.

Furthermore, it is unclear what Rothstein J. meant when he stated that this duty brings with it a lower threshold for breach than do Crown/Aboriginal fiduciary duties. The content of a Crown/Aboriginal fiduciary duty, post-*Haida Nation* and once triggered, is a mandate to act with reference to the best interest of an applicable Aboriginal group. Exactly how that mandate is intended to differ from the fundamental Crown honour mandate (to act honourably in dealings with an Aboriginal group) has been left unexplained.

My contention is that Rothstein J.'s evident confusion or resistance in relation to the fundamentals of the emergent honour of the Crown framework is a manifestation of the fact that the Supreme Court has not clearly acknowledged that its nonconventional approach to fiduciary accountability in Crown/Aboriginal contexts was, in effect, fundamentally adjusted in *Haida Nation*, if not jettisoned. Put plainly, Crown honour accountability

94 *Ibid.* at para. 208.

95 *Ibid.*

96 *Ibid.*

now does what Crown fiduciary accountability used to do, and there is no apparent residual role for a nonconventional type of Crown/Aboriginal fiduciary obligation (of the kind articulated in *Haida Nation*), despite the insistence to the contrary in both *Haida Nation* and *Manitoba Métis Federation*.

III

CONVENTIONAL FIDUCIARY LAW

> It is important to remember . . . that not every legal claim arising out of a per se fiduciary relationship . . . will give rise to a claim for a breach of fiduciary duty. . . . A claim for breach of fiduciary duty may only be founded on breaches of the specific obligations imposed because the relationship is one characterized as fiduciary.
>
> — Justice Cromwell in *Galambos* v. *Perez*[1]

TO CONCEPTUALIZE FIDUCIARY DOCTRINE GENERALLY AND THE SPECIFIC manner in which it has been used in Crown/Aboriginal contexts, initial questions one may pose are:

- What does it mean in Canada to say that an obligation is fiduciary in nature?
- What does it mean in Canada to say that a relationship is fiduciary in nature?

One would expect answers to these fundamental questions to be readily available in the applicable jurisprudence. Unfortunately, in both (a) *Guerin* and *Sparrow* (the two cases that principally incubated the Supreme Court's Crown/Aboriginal fiduciary doctrine), and (b) much of the academic commentary on the nature of Crown/Aboriginal fiduciary doctrine,[2] these

1 *Galambos* v. *Perez,* 2009 SCC 48, [2009] 3 S.C.R. 247 at paras. 36–37 [*Galambos* cited to S.C.R.].

2 See, e.g., Leonard Rotman, *Parallel Paths: Fiduciary Doctrine and the Crown-Native Relationship in Canada* (Toronto: University of Toronto Press, 1996); Brian Slattery, "First Nations and the Constitution: A Question of Trust" (1992) 71 Can. B. Rev. 261; James Reynolds, "The Spectre of Spectra: The Evo-

questions are dealt with in an oddly perfunctory manner. This dearth of analysis on fundamental principles is striking. Furthermore, the treatment of fiduciary doctrine in *Guerin* and *Sparrow* is novel and literally unprecedented; judicial precedent was not cited in support of the adoption of fiduciary doctrine in either case.[3]

Consequently, in this chapter I look to first principles — to conventional fiduciary law jurisprudence — in order to better conceptualize the nature of fiduciary accountability and the role it may or may not be equipped to play in Crown/Aboriginal contexts. It will be observed that the Supreme Court of Canada's conventional fiduciary law has, at least since *Guerin* (not coincidentally), been marked by quite extraordinary ill-resolve. Fiduciary law was described in a post-*Guerin* decision as "one of the most ill-defined, if not altogether misleading" areas of Canadian law.[4] While this complicates the task of conceptualizing how fiduciary accountability is to apply in Crown/Aboriginal contexts post-*Haida Nation,* a substantial measure of clarity has emerged through a recent line of Supreme Court decisions[5] and this clarity provides some assistance for the prject at hand.

Conventional fiduciary law in Canada has been described (at least since

---

lution of the Crown's Fiduciary Obligation to Aboriginal Peoples Since *Delgamuukw*" in Maria Morellato, QC (Ed.), *Aboriginal Law Since Delgamuukw* (Aurora: Canada Law Book, 2009); Kent McNeil, "The Crown's Fiduciary Obligations in the Era of Aboriginal Self-Government" (2009) 88 Can Bar Rev 1; and the various chapters in Law Commission of Canada, *In Whom We Trust: A Forum on Fiduciary Relationships* (Toronto: Irwin Law, 2002), particularly at 81–113 and 269–293.

3 In *Guerin* v. *The Queen*, [1984] 2 S.C.R. 335, 13 D.L.R. (4th) 321 at 384-385 [cited to S.C.R.], Dickson J. did cite two lower court decisions in support of one discreet principle related to fiduciary doctrine, but cited none in support of his novel interpretation of the main doctrinal fundamentals.

4 This comment was made by Justice La Forest J. in *Lac Minerals Ltd.* v. *International Corona Resources Ltd.* (1989), 61 D.L.R. (4th) 14, [1989] 2 S.C.R. 574 [*Lac Minerals* cited to S.C.R.] at 644, citing Professor Paul Finn.

5 *K.L.B.* v. *British Columbia*, [2003] 2 S.C.R. 403, 2003 SCC 5 [*KLB* cited to S.C.R.]; *Galambos, supra* note 1; and *Alberta* v. *Elder Advocates of Alberta Society*, 2011 SCC 24, [2011] 2 S.C.R. 261 at para. 44 [*Elder Advocates* cited to S.C.R.].

Guerin)[6] as a "profoundly confused jurisprudence"[7] and as following a theoretical approach consistent with "analytical nihilism," devoid of practical utility.[8] An extensive review of the Supreme Court of Canada jurisprudence[9] and of leading academic commentary[10] reveals that the funda-

---

6 As noted in Robert Flannigan, "Fact-Based Fiduciary Accountability in Canada," 36 Advocates' Q. 431 at 447: "*Guerin* is widely recognized as the decision that signaled the Canadian departure from conventional accountability, and the subsequent struggle to articulate boundaries."

7 Leonard I. Rotman, *Fiduciary Law* (Toronto: Thomson Carswell, 2005) at 20.

8 Matthew Conaglen, *Fiduciary Loyalty: Protecting the Due Performance of Non-Fiduciary Duties* (Oxford: Hart Publishing, 2010) at 26-28. See also, D.A. De Mott, "Fiduciary Obligation Under Intellectual Siege: Contemporary Challenges to the Duty to be Loyal," (1992) 30 Osgoode Hall L.J. 471 at 497.

9 *Midcon Oil & Gas Ltd.* v. *New British Dominion Oil Co.*, [1958] S.C.R. 314, 12 D.L.R. (2d) 705 [*Midcon* cited to S.C.R.]; *Peso Silver Mines Ltd.* v. *Cropper*, [1966] S.C.R. 673, 58 D.L.R. (2d) 1 [*Peso Silver Mines* cited to S.C.R.]; *Hawrelak* v. *City of Edmonton*, [1976] 1 S.C.R. 387, 54 D.L.R. (3d) 45 [*Hawrelak*]; *Can. Aero* v. *O'Malley* [1974] S.C.R. 592, 40 D.L.R. (3d) 371 [*Can. Aero* cited to S.C.R.]; *Frame* v. *Smith*, [1987] 2 S.C.R. 99, 42 D.L.R. (4th) 81 [*Frame* cited to S.C.R.]; *Lac Minerals, supra* note 4; *Canson Enterprises Ltd.* v. *Boughton & Co.*, [1991] 3 S.C.R. 534, 85 D.L.R. (4th) 129 [*Canson* cited to S.C.R.]; *Norberg* v. *Wynrib*, [1992] 2 S.C.R. 224, [1992] 6 W.W.R. 673 [*Norberg* cited to S.C.R.]; *McInerney* v. *MacDonald*, [1992] 2 S.C.R. 138, 93 D.L.R. (4th) 415 [*McInerney* cited to S.C.R.]; *M.(K.)* v. *M.(H.)*, [1992] 3 S.C.R. 6 [1992] S.C.J. No. 85 (Q.L.) [*M.(K.)* v. *M.(H.)* cited to S.C.R.]; *Hodgkinson* v. *Simms*, [1994] 3 S.C.R. 377, [1994] S.C.J. No. 84 (Q.L.) [*Hodgkinson* cited to Q.L.]; *Soulos* v. *Korkontzilas*, [1997] 2 S.C.R. 217, 146 D.L.R. (4th) 214; *Cadbury Schweppes Inc.* v. *FBI Foods Ltd.*, [1999] 1 S.C.R. 142, 167 D.L.R. (4th) 577 at para. 30 [*Cadbury* cited to S.C.R.]; *KLB, supra* note 5; *Strother* v. *3464920 Canada Inc.*, [2007] 2 S.C.R. 177, 2007 SCC 24 [*Strother* cited to S.C.R.]; *Galambos, supra* note 1; *Elder Advocates, supra* note 5.

10 Notable works by leading theorists include: Rotman, *Fiduciary Law, supra* note 7; Conaglen, *Fiduciary Loyalty, supra* note 8; Tamar Frankel, *Fiduciary Law*, (Oxford: Oxford University Press, 2011), and the work of Flannigan which is set out in a series of articles including but not limited to: Robert Flannigan, "The Fiduciary Obligation," Oxford J. Legal Studies (1989) 9 (3): 285-322; Robert Flannigan, "The Boundaries of Fiduciary Accountability" (2004) 83 Can. B. Rev. 35; Robert Flannigan, "Access or Expectation: The Test for Fiduciary Accountability," 89(1) Can. B. Rev. 1 (2010); and Robert Flannigan, "The Core Nature of Fiduciary Accountability" [2009] N.Z. L. Rev. 375.

mentals of conventional fiduciary law in Canada (a) became substantially obscured post-*Guerin,* (b) remained unresolved for many years (and still are, to some extent), and (c) were substantially reconceptualized (and repaired) in a recent line of Supreme Court decisions.[11]

There are a host of competing theories among commentators (and Supreme Court Justices) on what fiduciary law is, and ought to be, all about. Viewing the broad selection of theories and pronouncements, fiduciary law in Canada may be understood, at a high level of abstraction, as a competition between two distinct schools of thought.

On the one hand, there are those who see the fiduciary concept as involving a singular prohibition against self-interested conduct — or the appearance of such — in applicable trust-based relationships.[12] On the other hand, there are those who conceptualize the fiduciary concept as more centrally structured around a general principle operating to source a range of tailored and specific fiduciary obligations in the distinctive contexts of applicable trust-based relationships.[13] Proponents of this latter approach would require of fiduciaries not the mere avoidance of self-interested conduct but exemplary moral conduct generally in the managing of interests under their trust and care.[14] When referring to the dynamics of this approach, commentators and courts often speak in terms of it having constituted an expansive approach to fiduciary doctrine, as having expanded the conventional boundaries.

The fundamental distinction between these two approaches is not so much one of degree (i.e., of just how much the boundaries expand) but is, rather, one of fundamental jurisprudential form. The first school of thought is organized around a fiduciary rule: those in trust-based relationships shall not act or appear to act in self-interest regarding the incidents of a trust reposed. The second school of thought is organized around a fiduciary principle: those in trust-based relationships are to act honestly and

11 See the cases cited at *supra* note 5.

12 Leading proponents of this approach include Flannigan and Conaglen. See, e.g., Flannigan, "The Boundaries of Fiduciary Accountability," *supra* note 10; and Conaglen, *Fiduciary Loyalty*, *supra* note 8.

13 Rotman is a leading academic proponent of this approach: see, e.g., *Fiduciary Law, supra* note 7 generally, and at 295 specifically. La Forest J. was the leading judicial proponent of this approach in Canada, as further discussed below.

14 See, e.g., Rotman, *Fiduciary Law, supra* note 7 at 18.

with high honour and integrity in relation to the trust interests reposed.

Recall from Chapter One that in accordance with the applicable Dworkinian terminology, rules operate in all-or-nothing fashion (i.e., if the facts a rule stipulates are present, liability necessarily follows), whereas principles operate in a distinctly different jurisprudential manner. Principles incline a decision one way or another but do not by their form dictate specific results; rather, principles give rise to specific rights and rules in different contexts.[15]

Throughout the remainder of this book, where I make reference to these two schools of thought, I distinguish them for convenience as, respectively, a rule-based conception of fiduciary accountability and a principle-based conception of fiduciary accountability.

There is some debate as to whether fiduciary accountability, historically, was more of a rule-based or a principle-based concept.[16] Flannigan points to a number of eighteenth-century precedents to argue that "from the beginning of its recorded history," it was essentially a legal construct consistent with the rule-based conception, a fully independent doctrine that operated solely to control the self-regarding impulse of actors in trust-based relationships and which operated in parallel to other legal duties.[17] Professor Matthew Conaglen, alternatively, disputes the certainty of Flannigan's position and argues that much is lost in translation in some of the earliest applicable judgements, and that "the historical evidence cannot be said to be completely compelling one way or the other."[18]

Professor Leonard Rotman, for his part, describes fiduciary doctrine historically (and normatively in the contemporary context) in a manner more consistent with the principle-based conception, suggesting it was always less concerned with the prohibition of a singular type of behaviour than with the protection of important societal relationships generally, and with

---

15 Ronald Dworkin, *Taking Rights Seriously* (Cambridge: Harvard University Press, 1977) at 24-35.

16 See, e.g., Conaglen, *Fiduciary Loyalty*, *supra* note 8 at 11-31; Rotman, *Fiduciary Law, supra* note 7 at 153-237; Frankel, *Fiduciary Law, supra* note 10 at 79-101; and J. Getzler, "Rumford Market and the Genesis of Fiduciary Obligations," in Andrew Burrows and Lord Rodger of Earlsferry (Eds.), *Mapping the Law: Essays in Memory of Peter Birks* (Oxford: Oxford University Press, 2006).

17 See Robert Flannigan, "Book Review: A Romantic Conception of Fiduciary Obligation," 84 Can. B. Rev. 391 at 396.

18 Conaglen, *Fiduciary Loyalty*, *supra* note 8 at 18.

controlling the general manner in which those in positions of trust acted in relation to entrusted interests. Rotman argues that fiduciary accountability in its historical and contemporary essence involves a mandate requiring fiduciaries to "act with honesty, selflessness, integrity, fidelity and in the utmost good faith (*uberrima fides*) in the interests of their beneficiaries."[19]

However, in contrast to (and, indeed, in explicit opposition to[20]) Rotman's thesis, and regardless of the debate on the nature of historical precedent, Conaglen and Flannigan (and other leading commentators[21]) generally agree that as the jurisprudence evolved throughout the commonwealth, fiduciary law became (if it was not already) predominantly concerned with strictly, if not exclusively, prohibiting self-interested behaviour in trust and trust-like contexts. The jurisprudence is not uniform, but this general conceptualization of its central, long-standing proscription is ubiquitous.

At a high level, it can be said that the core construct of conventional fiduciary doctrine, on which there is relatively broad consensus among jurists, is essentially as follows: where a beneficiary in a trust or trust-like relationship is able to establish that his or her alleged fiduciary acted, or appeared to act, without consent,[22] in a self-regarding manner regarding trust interests reposed, strict liability follows and extraordinary remedial flexibility attends. The beneficiary need not have suffered any harm and the alleged fiduciary need not have acted dishonestly or with ill intent.[23]

While an extensive review of the different types of remedies available

19 Rotman, *Fiduciary Law, supra* note 7 at 18.

20 See, e.g., Conaglen's rejection of Rotman's proposed approach in Conaglen, *Fiduciary Loyalty, supra* note 8 at 106-113. Flannigan, for his part, has also directly confronted Rotman's approach: see, e.g., Flannigan, "A Romantic Conception of Fiduciary Obligation," *supra* note 17.

21 See, as two examples among many, Joshua Getzler, "Duty of Care" in Peter Birks and Arianna Pretto (Eds.), *Breach of Trust* (Oxford: Hart Publishing, 2002) at 41; and Ernest J. Weinrib, "The Fiduciary Obligation" (1975) 25 U.T.L.J. 1.

22 Consent is a full defence to an allegation of breach. See, e.g., *Midcon, supra* note 9 at 327; *Peso Silver Mines, supra* note 9 at 680; *Can. Aero, supra* note 9 at 607; *Hodgkinson, supra* note 9 at para. 88.

23 See, e.g., *Midcon, supra* note 9 at 337; and *Peso Silver Mines, supra* note 9 at 680.

for a fiduciary breach is beyond the scope of this book,[24] the governing remedial precepts are both restitutionary and punitive, and are generally seen as more generous to claimants than those that attend a breach of any other obligation known to law. A beneficiary need not prove damages (the applicable remedy can be gain-based as opposed to damages-based[25]) and windfalls to a beneficiary are permissible because furtherance of the deterrence objective takes priority. Wherever a fiduciary has derived profit in a position of conflict or has diverted profit to a non-arms-length third party — again, even where a beneficiary does not suffer loss — strict disgorgement in favour of the beneficiary is the classic order.

The long-accepted policy rational for the strictness, or bluntness, of fiduciary regulation is that fiduciary breaches in trust-based relationships may be uniquely tempting for fiduciaries, difficult to prove and to regulate, and uniquely easy to conceal.[26] It is also often suggested that the strict prohibition was, in part, born of a societal desire to deal harshly with faithless conduct generally in relationships that society places a particular value on nurturing and protecting.[27]

While this brief summary of conventional fiduciary doctrine may seem clear enough, it will soon become apparent as I move to a detailed examination of the Supreme Court of Canada jurisprudence that (a) it is imbued with several analytical landmines that have led to uncertainty (the prime example being the notoriously intractable problem of identifying a test for the types of societal interactions that attract fiduciary accountability), and (b) the Supreme Court, while not disputing a strict prohibition against self-interested conduct as a central feature of fiduciary law (and, to be clear, only one Supreme Court of Canada decision outside the Crown/Aboriginal context has ever enforced any other type of fiduciary breach[28]), has at times described its

24 On remedies for breaches of fiduciary obligations, see, generally, Mark Vincent Ellis, *Fiduciary Duties in Canada*, v.2 (Toronto: Thomson Reuters, 2004) at 20–21.

25 See, e.g., *Can. Aero, supra* note 9 at 612, 622–623; and *Midcon, supra* note 9 at 338.

26 See, e.g., *Midcon, supra* note 9 at 337; *Canson, supra* note 9 at 544; and *Frame, supra* note 9 at 137.

27 See, e.g., *Hodgkinson, supra* note 9 at para. 48; and Rotman, *Fiduciary Law, supra* note 7 at 259–260.

28 Flannigan made this point in “The Boundaries of Fiduciary Accountability,”

doctrine in much broader terms, terms capable of wildly varying interpretations; the latter a fact the jurisprudence has generally borne out.

Until recently, the Supreme Court's post-*Guerin* conventional fiduciary law reads as a confused blend of the rule-based and principle-based approaches articulated above. Interestingly, at a point where the Supreme Court's doctrine was particularly unsettled, the sitting Chief Justice of the British Columbia Court of Appeal delivered a strongly worded indictment of the failure of the Supreme Court of Canada to "make the law as clear as it should be" in this area.[29] In the following passage from *C.A.* v. *Critchley*, McEachern C.J.B.C. refers to the Supreme Court's effective shift to a principle-based approach as an experiment and pleads with them to revert back to a rule-based approach:

> Until recently, [fiduciary doctrine] was used for the purpose of requiring disloyal agents to disgorge secret or unlawful profits. Quite recently, fiduciary law has been extended to cover a myriad of circumstances. . . . Our Supreme Court of Canada has led the way in the common law world in extending fiduciary responsibilities . . . but it has not provided as much guidance as it usually does in emerging areas of law . . .. it is time, in my view, for the law to be made more certain and less subjective. Certainly I regard it as part of this Court's responsibility to urge the Supreme Court of Canada to clarify the law. . . . *Guerin* is obviously a case that should be confined to its particular facts and we should not be timid. . . . I conclude that it would be a principled approach to confine recovery . . . to cases of the kind where . . . the defendant personally takes advantage of a relationship of trust or confidence for his or her direct or indirect personal advantage. . . . In effect, this redirects fiduciary law back towards where it was before this experiment began. . . .[30]

It was for similarly framed reasons that the New South Wales Court of Appeal stated that "Canadian authorities on equity must be treated with

---

supra note 10 at 65.

29 *C.A.* v. *Critchley*, [1998] B.C.J. No. 2587 (Q.L.), 166 D.L.R. (4th) 475 at para. 79 [*Critchley* cited to D.L.R.].

30 *Ibid.* at paras. 74–75, 84–85.

considerable caution."[31]

Against this overall backdrop, I move now to a closer examination of the jurisprudence. The following analysis of conventional fiduciary law in the Supreme Court of Canada is set at a relatively high level of abstraction and organized around three incidents: (1) the function of fiduciary law; (2) the general content of fiduciary accountability (specifically, the nature of fiduciary obligations and fiduciary breaches); and (3) the specific trust-based contexts in which fiduciary accountability arises.

a. Function of fiduciary accountability

The core function of fiduciary law in Canada is difficult to isolate; the Supreme Court of Canada "has refused to tie its hands"[32] in terms of (explicitly) committing to a discernible mandate. It has been stated that the judicial disarray generally in this area (both in Canada and to the extent it exists in jurisprudence elsewhere) is primarily a result of a lack of clarity on the applicable function.[33] Accordingly, this is my starting point.

There are various instances in the jurisprudence where the Supreme Court of Canada has sought to articulate a general function (or functions) for fiduciary law. But instead of consensus, there are various incompatible or overlapping pronouncements. Evident in the case law are (at least) five distinct types of function that have in various decisions been posited for fiduciary law:

1. To regulate against self-interested behaviour (or opportunism) by trustees or by those acting in trustee-like roles;[34]
2. To promote the due performance of applicable non-fiduciary

31 *Harris v. Digital Pulse Pty Ltd* [2003] N.S.W.C.A. 10 at 32, (2003) 56 N.S.W.L.R. 298, cited in Conaglen, *Fiduciary Loyalty, supra* note 8 at 25.

32 *Lac Minerals, supra* note 4 at 296.

33 See, e.g., Flannigan "The Boundaries of Fiduciary Accountability," *supra* note 10 at 36; and Conaglen, *Fiduciary Loyalty, supra* note 8 at 26.

34 See, e.g., *KLB, supra* note 5 at para. 33. Implicitly, this seems to be the function predominantly observed throughout the jurisprudence, though when the Supreme Court has taken occasion to explicitly articulate a central function for the area, it has often done so in different terms.

duties by trustees or by those acting in trustee-like roles;[35]

3. To maintain the integrity of social and economic relationships that society places particular value on;[36]
4. To promote norms of exemplary behaviour in trust-based relationships;[37] and
5. To generally monitor or supervise the manner in which a trustee (or person in a trustee-like capacity) exercises his or her discretion regarding applicable interests entrusted to them.[38]

Flannigan posits that the singular function of fiduciary law is and has always been the control of opportunism in applicable arrangements.[39] He argues that all the other ways in which the Supreme Court has sought to articulate function are each open to misinterpretation, and that only by understanding fiduciary law's function as the control of opportunism can we be sure that it remains focussed on the singular mischief it seeks to control.

Rotman, in contrast, sees fiduciary law serving a distinctly different type of function. He sees it as having much in the way of untapped potential,[40] and he interprets the overall jurisprudence (historical and contemporary) as ultimately standing for the proposition that the primary function of fiduciary law is to protect the types of relationships that make society a better place. Rotman states:

> The interest and concern that the fiduciary concept has generated may be traced to the important purpose that it is designed to fulfill. "Fiduciary" is one of the means by which law transmits its ethical resolve to the spectrum of human interaction . . . its purpose is to preserve important

---

35 See, e.g., *Hodgkinson, supra* note 9 at 82; *Elder Advocates, supra* note 5 at para. 43; and *Strother, supra* note 9 at para. 83.

36 See, e.g., *Hodgkinson, supra* note 9 at paras. 48 and 93; *Galambos, supra* note 1 at para. 70.

37 See, e.g., *Can. Aero, supra* note 9 at 306.

38 See, e.g., *Guerin, supra* note 3 at 385; and *Hodgkinson, supra* note 9 at para. 27.

39 See, e.g., Flannigan, "The Boundaries of Fiduciary Accountability," *supra* note 10 at 35.

40 See, e.g., L. I. Rotman, "Fiduciary Doctrine: A Concept in Need of Understanding" (1996) 34 Alta. L. Rev. 821 at 852.

> social and economic interactions. In particular, it is impressed with the difficult task of maintaining the integrity of socially and economically valuable, or necessary, relationships of high trust and confidence that facilitate and flow from human interdependency.[41]

The simple takeaway from this brief section is that the range of conduct that fiduciary law purports to regulate may well differ, depending on what is seen as the doctrine's central function. And the Supreme Court could add clarity to their doctrine by arriving at a consensus on function.

I now consider the substantive nature of a fiduciary obligation (and a fiduciary breach).

b. Content of fiduciary duties

Fundamentally, and as noted above, fiduciary accountability is said to involve a strict obligation placed upon actors in applicable trust-based relationships to avoid both (a) self-interested behaviour, and (b) the appearance of self-interested behaviour. This is the most common conception of fiduciary accountability.[42]

In one of the early Supreme Court of Canada decisions addressing fiduciary accountability, Rand J., in a dissenting judgement, states that the general nature of fiduciary accountability "has been laid down consistently for several centuries"[43] and may be generally understood as follows:

> The loyalty of a fiduciary . . . means that he must divest himself of all thought of personal interest or advantage that impinges adversely on the interest of the beneficiary or that result from the use, in any manner or degree by the fiduciary, of the property, interest or influence of the beneficiary. . . . The fiduciary relation is that of trust in one who is to act in relation to the beneficial interest of another. It creates a standard of loyalty that calls for . . . the exclusion of all personal advantage

41 Rotman, *Fiduciary Law, supra* note 7 at 2 and 259.

42 See, e.g., *KLB, supra* note 5 at para. 48; *Hodgkinson, supra* note 9 at 96-97; and *Peso Silver Mines, supra* note 9 at 680.

43 *Midcon, supra* note 9 at 336 (*per* Rand J. in his dissenting opinion).

> and the total avoidance of any personal involvement in the interests being served or protected. . . .[44]

The content of fiduciary accountability is often described as a prohibition against both profit and conflict (conflict of interest or conflict of duty) in the carrying out of one's trust-based undertakings.[45] Indeed, the related concepts of profit and conflict have often been posited as the only two legitimate forms of fiduciary breach.[46] The content of fiduciary accountability, understood as such, fits nicely into a rule-based construct (i.e., if a fiduciary actor self-deals, or appears to self-deal, in the circumstances of their trust-based undertakings, she or he commits a fiduciary breach and liability necessarily follows — in accordance with the bluntness of the classic, strict rule).

However, and as indicated above, the Supreme Court of Canada has often described the content of fiduciary accountability in terms consistent with it being conceptualized more as a principle-based construct. The first instance of the Supreme Court departing somewhat from the conventional rule-based approach (by using language consistent with a principle-based approach) appear in the 1974 decision of *Can. Aero*, where Laskin J. states that fiduciary accountability "in its generality betokens loyalty, good faith, and the avoidance of a conflict of duty and self-interest" and that it seeks to "compel obedience . . . to norms of exemplary behaviour."[47] Note that this *dictum* departs from the classic rule-based construct described above, suggesting that bad faith generally or conduct constituting less than "exemplary behaviour" may conceivably constitute a fiduciary breach. The implication on a plain reading of this language, notwithstanding the fact it is not otherwise apparent in *Can Aero* that Laskin J. intended as much, is that fiduciary actors may have prescriptive fiduciary obligations to act in good faith, loyally, and in exemplary fashion; that fiduciary accountability is not necessarily limited to the proscriptive prohibition against self-dealing (i.e., profit and conflict).

Following *Can. Aero*, the next major shift toward a principle-based approach came in *Guerin* and the Crown/Aboriginal line of cases which, as dis-

---

44 *Ibid.* at 335 and 342 (*per* Rand J. in his dissenting opinion).

45 See, e.g., *Lac Minerals, supra* note 4 at 646–647.

46 See, e.g., Conaglen, *Fiduciary Loyalty, supra* note 8 at 32–58.

47 *Can. Aero, supra* note 9 at 306.

cussed in detail in the next chapter, ultimately recognized the Crown as under a fiduciary obligation "to treat Aboriginal people fairly and honourably."[48] Again, a prescriptive fiduciary obligation to act fairly and honourably is a far distance removed from a tractable rule-based standard, and quite distinct from the classic fiduciary prohibition against self-dealing.

Although Dickson J. may have been concerned to limit his novel fiduciary analysis in *Guerin* to Crown/Aboriginal contexts, having described the fiduciary obligation he observed as owing in the circumstances of that case as *sui generis* in nature,[49] *Guerin* was distinctly influential in shaping the future development of conventional fiduciary law in Canada.[50]

The Supreme Court Justice most responsible for propelling the court toward a principle-based approach to fiduciary accountability was Justice La Forest, who repeatedly referred in applicable decisions to the development of a "fiduciary principle," a process he viewed as having began in *Guerin*.[51]

In *Lac Minerals,* Justice La Forest stated of fiduciary accountability that "compendiously it can be described as the fiduciary duty of loyalty and will most often include the avoidance of a conflict of duty and interest and a duty not to profit at the expense of the beneficiary."[52] Like Laskin J. in *Can. Aero,* La Forest J. in this *dictum* describes the prohibition against conflict and profit as the most common but not exclusive type of fiduciary mandate.

As noted above, while many Supreme Court of Canada decisions subsequent to *Guerin* describe fiduciary accountability as potentially regulating more than self-interested behaviour, only one case outside the Crown/Aboriginal context actually finds and enforces a fiduciary breach that does not, in effect, take the form of a conflict or profit, and that decision was written by Justice La Forest.

In *McInerney*, the Supreme Court held that a doctor owed a patient a fi-

48 *Mitchell* v. *M.N.R.,* [2001] 1 S.C.R. 911, 2001 SCC 33 at para. 9 [cited to S.C.R.].

49 *Guerin, supra* note 3 at 387.

50 As noted by Flannigan, for instance, in "Fact-Based Fiduciary Accountability in Canada," *supra* note 6 at 447: "*Guerin* is widely recognized as the decision that signaled the Canadian departure from conventional accountability, and the subsequent struggle to articulate boundaries."

51 See, e.g., *Hodgkinson, supra* note 9 at 29; and *M.(K.)* v. *M.(H.), supra* note 9 at para. 33.

52 *Lac Minerals, supra* note 4 at 646–647.

duciary obligation to inform his patient regarding the content of medical records the doctor had obtained from other medical professionals. Relying heavily on *Guerin*, La Forest conceptualizes fiduciary doctrine in *McInerney* as operating to supervise behaviour broadly[53] and generally posits that a fiduciary actor has an obligation to act in the best interests of their beneficiary.[54]

This notion that fiduciary accountability involves an obligation to act in the "best interests" of one's beneficiary, a notion germinated in *Guerin*, is one also picked up in other Supreme Court decisions.[55] Again, and unless this "best interests" mandate is interpreted as a singular duty to act in an other-regarding manner, such a conception of fiduciary accountability is a principle-based construct and not a rule-based construct (i.e., it is not a standard that identifies specific facts that necessitate liability in all cases).

Moving on, it was noted at the outset that despite the unsettled nature of the Supreme Court's conventional fiduciary law jurisprudence, there are some seeds of clarity emerging in a trend that can be traced through a recent line of decisions. In these decisions, the Supreme Court appears now to be distancing itself from its principle-based conception of the content of fiduciary accountability and attempting to develop a more restrictive account of relationship regulation, one more consistent with a rule-based construct.

In *KLB*, it had been argued that lack of care by government officials in their act of placing the plaintiff children in foster homes (which led to the plaintiff being sexually assaulted in those homes) was a fiduciary breach in that it constituted a failure to act in the best interests of the children involved. McLachlin C.J. ultimately disagreed, explaining that there was "no evidence that the government put its own interests ahead of those of the children or committed acts that harmed the children in a way that amounted to betrayal of trust or disloyalty. . . [the] fault was not disloyalty [and so not a fiduciary breach] but failure to take sufficient care."[56]

Moreover, she stated that the specific fiduciary obligation that existed in the facts of this case was an obligation to "act loyally, and not to put one's own or others' interests ahead of the child's in a manner that abused the

53 *McInerney, supra* note 9 at 149.

54 *Ibid.* at 154.

55 See, e.g., *Norberg, supra* note 9 and *Hodgkinson, supra* note 9, generally.

56 *KLB, supra* note 5 at para. 50.

child's trust."[57]

In her decision, the Chief Justice goes to some length to reject the notion that a duty to act in the best interests of a beneficiary is properly viewed as fiduciary in nature. Her rejection is made on two bases: first, she states that a fiduciary-based best-interests ethic lacks practical utility in the sense that it fails to provide a "workable standard by which to regulate conduct . . . [that it] simply does not provide a legal or justiciable standard";[58] second, she states that it leads to an inappropriate result-based analysis, explaining in the circumstances of the case that

> Parents should try to act in the best interests of their children. . . . However, thus far, failure to meet this goal has not itself been elevated to an independent ground of liability at common law or equity. There are good reasons for this . . . an obligation to do what is in the best interests of one's child would seem to be a form of result-based liability, rather than liability based on faulty actions and omissions: such an obligation would be breached whenever the result was that the best interests of the child were not promoted, regardless of what steps had or had not been taken by the parent. Breach of fiduciary duty, however, requires fault.[59]

This *dictum* from *KLB* reflects a recent trend involving an attempt by the Supreme Court to make clear, in the words of Justice Binnie in *Wewaykum* (a decision released shortly before *KLB*), that "not all obligations existing between the parties to a fiduciary relationship are themselves fiduciary in nature."[60] A similar comment, included as part of the epigraph to this chapter, is made by Justice Cromwell in *Galambos*: "[a] claim for breach of fiduciary duty may only be founded on breaches of the specific obligations imposed because the relationship is one characterized as fiduciary."[61]

Moreover, this recent trend closely mirrors *dictum* from a leading Eng-

57 *Ibid.* at para. 34.

58 *Ibid.* at para. 46.

59 *Ibid.* at 44-45.

60 *Wewaykum Indian Band* v. *Canada,* [2002] 4 S.C.R. 245, 220 D.L.R. (4th) 1 at para. 83 [cited to S.C.R.].

61 *Galambos, supra* note 1 at para. 37.

lish decision on the nature of fiduciary accountability, *Bristol & West Building Society* v. *Mothew*, where Millet L.J. states that:

> The expression "fiduciary duty" is properly confined to those duties which are peculiar to fiduciaries and the breach of which attracts legal consequences differing from those consequent upon the breach of other duties. Unless the expression is so limited it is lacking in practical utility. In this sense it is obvious that not every breach of duty by a fiduciary is a breach of fiduciary duty.[62]

The question for present purposes then becomes: what are the specific types of breach of duty that are uniquely fiduciary in nature? In the two most recent Supreme Court of Canada decisions, both McLachlin C.J. (in *Elder Advocates*) and Cromwell J. (in *Galambos*) continue to resist restricting fiduciary accountability entirely to the classic prohibition against self-interested behaviour (or the appearance of such), instead placing central emphasis on abuse of power (McLachlin C.J. uses the similar if not synonymous notion abuse of trust) as the type of wrong that is fiduciary in nature. Further, abuse of power (or abuse of trust) is now isolated, at least temporarily, as the exclusive type of mischief regulated by conventional fiduciary law in Canada.

Put another way, the Supreme Court's current conceptualization of fiduciary accountability is as follows: an abuse of power (or trust) is the only recognized and actionable breach of the fiduciary duty of loyalty.

In *KLB*, Chief Justice McLachlin states the "emphasis" in terms of the content of a fiduciary "abuse of trust" is "disloyalty and promotion of one's own or others' interest at the expense of the beneficiary's interests."[63]

Ultimately, then, the Supreme Court has gone some distance to restrict its doctrine to a more rule-based conception of fiduciary accountability (arguably, a return to the classic fiduciary construct); that is, one that stipulates that if a fiduciary actor commits an abuse of power or trust in the context of their trust-based undertakings, liability necessarily follows. This is certainly a more restricted standard than a principle-based directive essentially mandating that fiduciaries act in accordance with a high standard of moral conduct generally. However, the terms "abuse of power" and "abuse

62 [1998] Ch. 1 (C.A.) at 16.

63 *KLB, supra* note 5 at para. 33.

of trust" are still clearly open to varying interpretations (despite McLachlin C.J.'s comment in *Elder Advocates* that the "emphasis" is to be on the prohibition of self-dealing[64]), and still, to some extent, beg the question: what specific types of power or trust abuses are uniquely fiduciary in nature?

In one of the most recent treatises attempting to theorize commonwealth fiduciary doctrine, Conaglen picks up on this question of what types of duties are peculiarly fiduciary in nature, delineates the main types of duties that have at times been held to be fiduciary in nature, discusses each at length, and posits in conclusion that only duties to avoid conflict and profit are properly characterized as fiduciary.[65]

It remains to be seen if the Supreme Court of Canada will follow suit, or if their concept of abuse of power (or abuse of trust) will apply more broadly. Though it is unclear whether the Supreme Court will land, fundamentally, on a principle-based or a rule-based construct (or, perhaps, persist on an opaque blend of the two), the trend seems to be a move toward restoration of the conventional rule-based approach.

c. Contexts in which fiduciary duties arise

I have now noted material uncertainty in two key incidents of the Supreme Court's doctrine on fiduciary law: (a) the core function (i.e., does fiduciary law function solely to control the self-regarding impulse of actors in trust-based relationships, or is it more fundamentally concerned with promoting a high standard of moral conduct generally?), and (b) the content of the mandate (i.e., is fiduciary accountability broader than a prohibition against conflict and profit?). I will now consider the various types of contexts in which fiduciary obligations are said to arise.

The original factual context in which fiduciary accountability first arose was the express trust. Because a trustee is given direct (and typically unmonitored) access to the assets or opportunities of a beneficiary on a mandate of managing those assets/opportunities in the best interests of that beneficiary, there is seen to be a unique opportunity for that trustee to act selfishly regarding those assets or opportunities, and in circumstances also seen as uniquely difficult to regulate. For that reason, and to reiterate, an

64 *Ibid.*

65 Conaglen, *Fiduciary Loyalty*, *supra* note 8 at 32–58.

equitable and uniquely strict rule — the fiduciary obligation — developed to prohibit even the appearance of self-dealing in such contexts.

The fiduciary obligation has since been applied in a wide variety of categories of human interaction/relationship. The following are some examples of relationship categories that have been found by various courts to be sufficiently trust-like so as to give rise, as a matter of course, to applicable fiduciary obligations:

- Executor-beneficiary
- Solicitor-client
- Agent-principal
- Director-corporation (and director-shareholder)
- Guardian-ward
- Doctor-patient
- Parent-child
- Elected official-electorate[66]

Beginning in its decision in *Lac Minerals*, the Supreme Court began to follow the practice of simply deeming that fiduciary accountability exists *per se* in the context of these types of traditionally-recognized categories of relationship, focussing the analysis in such contexts then on the types of conduct within such relationships that constitute a breach of fiduciary accountability owed.

Courts are often faced with (a) an allegation of a breach of a fiduciary obligation in circumstances that do not fall within one of the above-noted traditional categories of fiduciary relationship, or (b) an allegation that an alleged fiduciary's impugned conduct, while within the context of a relationship of a kind traditionally recognized as fiduciary in nature, is not a breach of duty that is itself fiduciary in nature. It is in these types of situations that attempts have been made to formulate a rationale to justify (or

---

66 When the traditional categories are delineated — as they often are — in Supreme Court decisions, this last relationship category (elected official-electorate) is inexplicably left off the list. However, although it rarely rises, this has been a long-recognized category of fiduciary relationship in Canada and elsewhere: see, e.g., "Governmental Authorities," Chapter 19 in Ellis, *Fiduciary Duties in Canada, supra* note 24 at 19-1; Robert Flannigan, "Fiduciary Control of Political Corruption" (2002) 26 Advocates' Q. 252 at 252; and the Supreme Court of Canada's decision in *Hawrelak, supra* note 9.

not) extending the scope of fiduciary accountability to a novel set of facts.

In order to determine whether or not fiduciary obligations ought to be extended to a new type of relationship category or factual situation, courts in various jurisdictions (as well as academic commentators) have struggled mightily to conceptualize what it is about the traditional categories of relationship that gives them their fiduciary quality (assuming that there must be a universal principle or rationale that unifies the various categories).

The Supreme Court of Canada, for its part, has been wildly inconsistent in its attempts to articulate the conceptual basis (or bases) upon which the classic trust-based fiduciary obligation has been (and ought to be) extended to other types of human interaction. As noted in the indictment of their jurisprudence by McEachern C.J.B.C. in *Critchley*, for instance, the Supreme Court's approach is seen by some as having been uniquely expansive.

Turning then to the applicable specifics of the Supreme Court's jurisprudence, it may be observed that beginning with its decision in *Guerin*, the Supreme Court developed numerous (effectively competing) tests and rationales for what ought to constitute the essential justification for the imposition of fiduciary accountability. Detailed analyses of some of the various tests and principles have been set out elsewhere.[67] In summary, what the Court initially attempted to isolate was an abstract indicator (or set of indicators) that would operate to determine, on a case-by-case basis, whether fiduciary obligations are indeed owed in any given context.

In *Guerin*, where fiduciary accountability was first used in the Crown/Aboriginal context, Justice Dickson offered this as the conceptual test for when fiduciary accountability arises:

> where by statute, agreement, or perhaps by unilateral undertaking, one party has an obligation to act for the benefit of another, and that obligation carries with it a discretionary power, the party thus empowered becomes a fiduciary.[68]

This oft-cited dictum from *Guerin* was later picked up by Justice Wilson

67 See, e.g., Flannigan "The Boundaries of Fiduciary Accountability," *supra* note 10 at 67–76; Leonard I. Rotman, "The Vulnerable Position of Fiduciary Doctrine in the Supreme Court of Canada," (1996) 24 Man. L.J. 60–91.

68 *Guerin, supra* note 3 at 384.

in *Frame* who went on to set out a "rough and ready guide to whether or not the imposition of a fiduciary obligation on a new relationship would be appropriate and consistent" in context.[69] Attempting to synthesize previous case law, she offered a flexible conceptual framework, essentially stating that fiduciary accountability would be appropriate in circumstances where some or all of the following three characteristics are present:

1. The fiduciary has scope for the exercise of some discretion or power.
2. The fiduciary can unilaterally exercise that power or discretion so as to affect the beneficiary's legal or practical interests.
3. The beneficiary is peculiarly vulnerable to or at the mercy of the fiduciary holding the discretion or power.[70]

Wilson J.'s "rough and ready guide" from *Frame* is widely cited in subsequent Supreme Court decisions. Various Supreme Court Justices sought to put their own spin on how Wilson J.'s guide should be applied. Justice La Forest, for instance, was a proponent of the view that the determinative question should be whether a claimant's expectation that a defendant ought to have acted in his or her best interests in the circumstances at issue was reasonable or legitimate (i.e., a reasonable/legitimate expectations test).[71] In contrast, Chief Justice McLachlin, in earlier decisions, saw as more centrally determinative the question of whether power or discretion was ceded by a claimant (explicitly or implicitly) to such an extent that the defendant was in a position to adversely affect the interests of the claimant (i.e., a power-ceding test).[72]

More recently, however, the Supreme Court has fundamentally changed course. In *Galambos* and *Elders Advocates*, the Supreme Court has effectively rejected the *Frame* approach of using flexible, abstract criteria (along with the reasonable-expectations and power-ceding tests of La Forest J.

69 As it was later described by Justice La Forest in *Lac Minerals, supra* note 4 at 647.

70 *Frame, supra* note 9 at 136.

71 See, e.g., *Lac Minerals, supra* note 4 at 648; and *Hodgkinson, supra* note 9 at para. 38.

72 See, e.g., *Hodgkinson, supra* note 9 at paras. 117-137 (*per* McLachlin J., as she then was, and Sopinka J.).

and McLachlin C.J., noted above) and has embraced more of an essentialist approach (i.e., one which holds that for fiduciary accountability to arise, certain essential facts must be present).

The current three-part Supreme Court of Canada test for when fiduciary accountability arises, as articulated by Chief Justice McLachlin in *Elder Advocates*, is as follows:

> 1. First, the evidence must show that the alleged fiduciary gave an undertaking of responsibility to act in the best interests of a beneficiary;
> 2. Second, the duty must be owed to a defined person or class of persons who must be vulnerable to the fiduciary in the sense that the fiduciary has a discretionary power over them; and
> 3. Finally . . . the claimant must show that the alleged fiduciary's power may affect the legal or substantial practical interests of the beneficiary. . . . [73] (footnotes omitted)

The first two components of the new test offer discernible boundaries of accountability, and are common features of the Supreme Court's conventional jurisprudence. For fiduciary accountability to arise, there must have been an undertaking by an alleged fiduciary to act in the best interests of a beneficiary, which undertaking may be explicit as in a statutory or contractual commitment, or implicit, as, for instance, self-evidently present in doctor-patient and parent-child relationships,[74] and the beneficiary must have been vulnerable in the sense that the alleged fiduciary had power or discretion in relation to their interests.

The third component, however, introduces a notion that will require further judicial elaboration. There is little guidance in the Supreme Court's jurisprudence on what types of interests, for instance, may be sufficiently vital or substantial to satisfy the third component of the test.[75]

---

73 *Elder Advocates, supra* note 5 at para. 36.

74 See, e.g., *Galambos, supra* note 1 at para. 75.

75 Generally, see Gordon D. Smith, "The Critical Resource Theory of Fiduciary Duty," 55 Vand. L. Rev. 1399 at 1444. See also Frankel, *Fiduciary Law, supra* note 10 at 13-25. For an argument that the criticality of the interests at issue is irrelevant to whether or not fiduciary accountability arises, see Robert Flannigan, "Fiduciary Mechanics" (2008) 14 C.L.E.L.J. 25 at 25-26, 46.

Before moving on, a current debate between two leading commentators is noteworthy here. Flannigan has long promoted the importance of following a strictly essentialist approach to the identification of conceptual boundaries of fiduciary accountability. For Flannigan, fiduciary accountability arises only (and always) when one person is entrusted with limited access to the assets or opportunities of another for a defined purpose.[76]

Conaglen, on the other hand, recently criticized Flannigan's model, and expressed doubts as to whether a truly essentialist or universal test for fiduciary accountability is possible, given the wide variety of social and factual contexts in which it is said to arise.[77] Conaglen (citing Canadian commentator Ernest J. Weinrib) noted the "notoriously intractable" task of isolating such a test.[78] Conaglen prefers a reasonable/legitimate expectations test of a kind earlier promoted by Justice La Forest (and one which allows recourse to the various types of abstract criteria noted above to have been used in the past by the Supreme Court) as the most intellectually satisfying of all available tests. He concedes the imperfect nature of this type of non-essentialist approach, but states that "courts have persevered with the concept, and the skies have not fallen."[79]

To the contrary, Flannigan has argued, metaphorically, that the skies in this area have fallen, explaining that a conceptual fog descended over the Supreme Court's fiduciary doctrine as a result of the non-essentialist approach they had chosen to follow post-*Guerin*.

Ultimately, while the Supreme Court has embraced a move to a more restricted, essentialist approach to the question of when fiduciary accountability arises, it remains to be seen how their new test will be applied by lower courts and, in particular, how the third component of the test — the interest in question being sufficiently vital or substantial — will be interpreted.

---

76 See, e.g., Flannigan, "The Boundaries of Fiduciary Accountability," *supra* note 10 at 36-54.

77 Conaglen, *Fiduciary Loyalty, supra* note 8 at 252 and 268.

78 Weinrib, "The Fiduciary Obligation," *supra* note 21 at 5, cited in Conaglen, *Fiduciary Loyalty, supra* note 8 at 9.

79 Conaglen, *Fiduciary Law, supra* note 8 at 261.

IV

FIDUCIARY LAW AS APPLIED, NONCONVENTIONALLY, IN CROWN/ABORIGINAL CONTEXTS

> In our opinion, *Guerin* [fiduciary obligations], together with *R.* v. *Taylor and Williams* [the honour of the Crown principle]. . . ground a general guiding principle for s.35(1). That is, the Government has the responsibility to act in a fiduciary capacity with respect to aboriginal peoples.
>
> — Chief Justice Dickson and Justice La Forest in *Sparrow*[1]

IN THE PREVIOUS CHAPTER, AT A HIGH LEVEL OF ABSTRACTION, I ARTICULATED two distinct and competing conceptualizations of fiduciary accountability — the principle-based (that the fiduciary concept is more a principle that gives rise to specific duties[2]), and the rule-based (that the fiduciary concept is a singular rule against self-interested conduct in applicable contexts) — and noted that the Supreme Court of Canada appears to be returning to a rule-based construct, after having experimented post-*Guerin* with a principle-based approach.[3]

---

1 *R.* v. *Sparrow*, [1990] 1 S.C.R. 1075, 70 D.L.R. (4th) 385 at 1108 [cited to S.C.R.].

2 Recall from the previous chapter that McEachern C.J.B.C. conceptualized this type of an approach as an ill-advised experiment in *C.A.* v. *Critchley*, [1998] B.C.J. No. 2587 (Q.L.), 166 D.L.R. (4th) 475 at paras. 79-85 [*Critchley* cited to D.L.R.].

3 Recall generally from the discussion above that Justice La Forest saw *Guerin* as effectively incubating a principle-based approach, and he was influential in

In this chapter, I examine the Supreme Court's nonconventional Crown/Aboriginal fiduciary doctrine. I track the key pronouncements, beginning with *Guerin* and *Sparrow*, and then contrast that thread of decisions with the more recent, transforming *dicta* in *Wewaykum* and *Haida Nation*. Following a general overview of the case law, I then proceed to a more detailed analysis following the same format as in the previous chapter on conventional fiduciary law by examining three discreet incidents of the Supreme Court's (evolving, but still nonconventional) Crown/Aboriginal fiduciary doctrine: its function, the content of the duties it is to include, and the specific Crown/Aboriginal contexts that give rise to it.

As will become clear, the Supreme Court appears to be, in decisions such as *Wewaykum* and *Haida Nation*, working toward an alignment of the fundamentals of its nonconventional Crown/Aboriginal fiduciary doctrine (which it had initially described as *sui generis* in nature[4]) with the core fundamentals of conventional fiduciary doctrine, itself a work in progress, as demonstrated in the last chapter. However, full alignment of the conventional and nonconventional is still a ways off.

Accepting the premise that the recent developments in the conventional jurisprudence mark a return to the roots of fiduciary law, one may begin to apprehend the difficulty of using conventional fiduciary law to regulate Crown conduct generally in Aboriginal contexts. That is, when Aboriginal and treaty rights come before a court, it is most often in the context of a societal friction between the interests of an Aboriginal or treaty rights-holder and the rights or interests of some other member or segment of society, or society writ large, of which the (often marginalized) Aboriginal rights holder is a part. In such contexts, the Crown is in a position of having to balance the various, often conflicting, interests involved with an eye toward some type of resolution; that is the essential function of its role. Consequently, they will not generally be seen as having undertaken to act exclusively in the best interests of anybody.[5] The Crown in such scenarios would typically not owe fiduciary obligations to any one party (Aboriginal or non-Aboriginal) with respect to the balancing of the applicable interests

---

reconceiving conventional fiduciary law on that basis.

4 *Guerin* v. *The Queen*, [1984] 2 S.C.R. 335, 13 D.L.R. (4th) 321 at 387 [cited to S.C.R.].

5 See, e.g., *Alberta* v. *Elder Advocates of Alberta Society*, 2011 SCC 24, [2011] 2 S.C.R. 261 at para. 44 [*Elder Advocates* cited to S.C.R.].

in dispute, pursuant to the Supreme Court's current test for when fiduciary accountability arises (i.e., their conventional doctrine).[6]

There are other instances of Crown/Aboriginal interaction, however (outside contexts that generally invoke a Crown mandate of reconciling Aboriginal or treaty rights with the interests of a third party or the overall citizenry), where fiduciary accountability clearly does arise in accordance with the prevailing, conventional doctrine.[7] The factual circumstances in the *Guerin* litigation are one such instance.

In the circumstances of *Guerin*, the Crown had undertaken, pursuant to its statutory mandate, to act exclusively in the best interests of the Musqueam when exercising its discretionary powers in the exercise of its mandate (i.e., of negotiating a fair deal with a third party for the land interest that the Musqueam had conditionally surrendered to the Crown for that purpose). In *Guerin*, that undertaking was part of the triggering criteria relied upon by Dickson J. to found fiduciary accountability, as it ought to have been.[8] Conventional fiduciary duties, based on any known conception, arose in that context. That is, the Crown and its agents were prohibited on the facts in *Guerin*, in accordance with conventional fiduciary doctrine, from acting in a self-interested manner in relation to the applicable Musqueam interests. That was the full extent of the conventional fiduciary obligation owed in that context.

Other instances where conventional fiduciary accountability arises in the context of Crown/Aboriginal interaction are situations like the one in *Ermineskin*,[9] where the Crown undertakes a statutory duty to manage resource royalty monies (i.e., royalties paid on resources extracted from Aboriginal lands) exclusively in the interests of an Aboriginal group. In those situations, there are clearly conventional fiduciary obligations that prohibit the Crown from, effectively, stealing the Aboriginal group's money.

---

6 See, generally, *Elder Advocates, ibid.* Note, however, that Crown actors often owe a conventional fiduciary duty to the electorate as a whole: see, e.g., Mark Vincent Ellis, *Fiduciary Duties in Canada*, v.2 (Toronto: Thomson Reuters, 2004) at chapter 19.

7 In accordance with the newly reconceptualized test for fiduciary accountability set out in *Elder Advocates, supra* note 5 at 36.

8 *Guerin, supra* note 4 at 385.

9 *Ermineskin Indian Band and Nation* v. *Canada* 2009 SCC 9, [2009] 1 S.C.R. 222 [cited to S.C.R.].

Notably, however, although conventional fiduciary obligations did arise in the circumstances of both the *Guerin* and *Ermineskin* cases, in neither case was there any real suggestion that such conventional fiduciary obligations (i.e., the rule against self-interested conduct) had been breached. While there was impugnable conduct in both instances, none took the form of a breach of a (properly conceptualized) conventional fiduciary obligation. In section (b)(i) of Chapter Six, I discuss what a breach of a conventional fiduciary obligation might actually look like in such contexts.

Moving on, and as already indicated, the Supreme Court's Crown/Aboriginal fiduciary doctrine was not developed in accordance with the conventional rule-based prohibition against self-interested conduct. Rather, it was brought in initially both to promote a high standard of moral conduct on the part of the Crown generally, and to regulate Crown dishonour in the context of the Crown's dealings with Aboriginal peoples in circumstances where there was the potential for Crown conduct to infringe or negatively affect Aboriginal or treaty rights (including Indian land interests), and it developed in accordance with a novel and distinctly principle-based approach.

To properly conceptualize the genesis of Crown/Aboriginal fiduciary doctrine in Canada, we must look closer at the circumstances surrounding the *Guerin* litigation. *Guerin* was the first Supreme Court of Canada decision to explicitly import fiduciary concepts into the core of Canadian Aboriginal law. In that case, the Supreme Court was addressing a situation where the Musqueam Band had leased a portion of their reserve lands to a third party for use as a golf course (the impugned conduct had taken place in the late 1950s). Pursuant to the *Indian Act*, the Musqueam had been required to first surrender the lands to the federal government, who then negotiated the lease with the third party on their behalf, on what was effectively a statutory undertaking to act exclusively in the Musqueam's best interests.[10]

Aboriginal peoples in Canada are typically precluded from disposing of their own lands to any entity other than the Crown, and the Crown for its part is then mandated to act on the behalf of the Aboriginal group in relation to those lands. This inalienability dynamic regarding Aboriginal peoples and their lands has always been a feature of Canadian constitutionalism (and remains to this day), and dates back to the *Royal Proclamation (1763)*,[11] where the Crown first formally assumed this type of responsibil-

10 *Guerin, supra* note 4 at 383–384.

11 Reprinted in R.S.C. 1985, App. II, No.1.

ity, and is now also codified in the *Indian Act*. The essential purpose of this arrangement, it has often been said, is the protection of Aboriginal peoples against "exploitative bargains" with settlers in relation to the disposition of their lands.[12]

What generally transpired in the circumstances of the *Guerin* case is that the federal Crown, in its dealings with the third party lessor, made some late adjustments to the terms of the lease that were never discussed with the Musqueam, adjustments that were deemed by the Crown to have been necessary to effect the deal but which made the transaction significantly less advantageous for the Musqueam. The Crown had failed to take into account, during their negotiations, certain concerns that the Band had previously raised with them, and once the lease was finalized, and despite repeated requests from the Band, the Musqueam were not shown a copy of the lease until approximately twelve years after it was signed.

It was not suggested on the facts of the case that the Crown acted out of self-interest. Rather, what was successfully argued, in essence, was that the Crown acted in too unilateral (or dishonourable) a fashion, that they ought to have gone back to the Musqueam to discuss the final negotiated adjustments to the lease before finalizing it, and that they should have worked harder to address some of the comments and concerns the Musqueam had raised in prior discussions with Crown officials regarding the lease, particularly since they had initially induced the Musqueam to avail themselves of the opportunity.[13]

This case was the first major Supreme Court decision to address the nature of Crown/Aboriginal obligations following the repatriation of the constitution in 1982, which, of course, saw Aboriginal and treaty rights recognized and affirmed. Prior to 1982, Crown responsibility in the context of Aboriginal lands was typically described as constituting a type of political trust (as opposed to a legal trust), and the Crown was effectively immune from judicial scrutiny regarding conduct relating to the administration of such lands. A notable line of early jurisprudence developed describing the nature of that form of Crown immunity.[14]

---

12 See, e.g., *Wewaykum Indian Band* v. *Canada*, [2002] 4 S.C.R. 245, 220 D.L.R. (4th) 1 at para. 100 [cited to S.C.R.].

13 *Guerin, supra* note 4 at 389.

14 For commentary, see Leonard I. Rotman, *Fiduciary Law* (Toronto: Thomson Carswell, 2005) at 562–565.

Predictably, therefore, there was substantial effort made in *Guerin* to conceptualize the resultant Crown/Musqueam relationship using trust language (indeed, the Musqueam had framed their claim in trust). For instance, and although Dickson J. declined to characterize that relationship as an express trust, finding rather that the relationship was trust-like and so attracted fiduciary accountability, Wilson J., in a minority decision, arrived at the conclusion that the relationship (between the Crown and the Musqueam, upon the surrender) was actually an express legal trust.[15]

On the facts, the Musqueam had argued that the Crown had failed to discharge its legal obligation in accordance with Musqueam best interests. Dickson J. ultimately agreed with that argument, concluding that the Crown had a fiduciary duty (but not a trust duty) in this scenario to act with "utmost loyalty" in the best interests of the Musqueam.[16]

Dickson J. did not, however, base his finding of fiduciary breach in the conventional way (i.e., on the Crown's conduct in putting its own interests in conflict with the applicable interests of the Musqueam). Rather, he conceptualized fiduciary law as operating to permit the Court, in circumstances where fiduciary accountability is recognized as having arisen (by the Crown having assumed a discretionary power to act exclusively on the Musqueam's behalf), to then flexibly monitor the entirety of the Crown's exercise of that discretion and to sanction perceived transgressions as breaches of the fiduciary duty to act loyally in the best interests of the Aboriginal group.

Dickson J. described the Crown conduct that had transpired in *Guerin* as unconscionable (seemingly conceiving unconscionability here in a plain sense of that word, since the conduct at issue would not have constituted conventional "unconscionability" at law,[17] nor was any such precedent cited to suggest it did). Dickson J. described his finding of unconscionability here as "the key to a conclusion that the Crown breached its fiduciary duty."[18]

Justice Dickson did not cite judicial authority in support of this concep-

---

15 *Guerin, supra* note 4 at 355.

16 *Ibid.* at 390.

17 As pointed out in Robert Flannigan, "The Boundaries of Fiduciary Accountability" (2004) 83 Can. B. Rev. 35 at 63.

18 *Guerin, supra* note 4 at 388.

tualization of the fundamental nature of fiduciary law.[19] He did refer more than once to the fiduciary obligation enforced in this case as *sui generis*,[20] which suggests he may well have been concerned about restricting his analysis to the specific facts of the case.

In radically varying the applicable doctrinal fundamentals, and without acknowledging that is what he was doing, Dickson J. arguably committed a conceptual error.[21] This forms the starting point of the broader argument I make in the next chapter that the Supreme Court's Crown/Aboriginal fiduciary doctrine in its entirety, and including its (adjusted) prevailing fundamentals in more recent decisions like *Haida Nation* and *Manitoba Métis Federation*, takes the form of a classic Dworkinian mistake.

Furthermore, it was not made clear in his reasons whether Dickson J. intended that the *sui generis* Crown/Aboriginal fiduciary accountability he recognized in *Guerin* would be confined to the facts of that case (i.e., Aboriginal land-surrender scenarios), or whether it was to apply more broadly in Crown/Aboriginal contexts. We know, from the discussion in the previous chapter, that his decision was applied broadly outside the Crown/Aboriginal context, effectively exported for a period of time to the core of conventional fiduciary doctrine.

Further, it was also, of course, extended to other forms of Crown/Aboriginal interaction. In *Sparrow*, Justice Dickson's account in *Guerin* was interpreted as a generalized fiduciary-based principle that Crown/Aboriginal relationships are fiduciary in nature and that the Crown is to act "in a fiduciary capacity" in all of its dealings involving Aboriginal and treaty rights, even those where the Crown has not undertaken a specific mandate of acting directly (and exclusively) in the interests of an Aboriginal group.

The *Sparrow* litigation involved a claim, again by the Musqueam, that in limiting the length of fishing nets that Band members could use (i.e., in the terms of the Band's food fishing license issued), the federal Crown had unconstitutionally infringed the exercise of Musqueam Aboriginal fishing rights. The Supreme Court did not make a determination in their decision

19 Dickson J. did cite two lower court decisions in support of one discreet principle related to fiduciary doctrine (*Guerin, supra* note 4 at 384–385) but none in support of his novel interpretation of the main doctrinal fundamentals.

20 *Guerin, supra* note 4 at 387.

21 Flannigan makes this argument in "The Boundaries of Fiduciary Accountability," *supra* note 17 at 63.

on whether the Crown conduct at issue constituted any type of breach of duty (fiduciary or otherwise) — the Court sent the matter back to trial for reconsideration of the liability issues — but they set out a detailed framework describing the manner in which Crown regulatory powers are restrained in instances where Aboriginal and treaty rights could potentially be affected.

The *Sparrow* Court confirmed that Aboriginal and treaty rights are not absolute, not immune from Crown regulation in contemporary society. However, they also confirmed that the constitutionalization of Aboriginal and treaty rights had the effect of placing material, legal constraints on applicable Crown (sovereign) regulatory powers. The Court held that any infringement of an Aboriginal or treaty right by Crown regulation must be justified in accordance with a detailed legal framework set out in the decision.

In describing the applicable justification test, the Court held that the legal restraint on Crown power constitutionalized in section 35 was fiduciary in nature.[22] Furthermore, and as noted in Chapter Two, where the Court sought to articulate a general ethic or constitutional principle that would ground applicable Crown obligations, it was held that the Crown had an obligation to generally act "in a fiduciary capacity" in relation to Aboriginal and treaty rights holders.

The main takeaway for present purposes is that *Sparrow* espoused a proposition, indeed a general constitutional principle, that any infringement of Aboriginal or treaty rights by the Crown in its regulatory function must be undertaken in accordance with a standard of conduct similar to that generally required of fiduciaries, mindful of the reality that there would typically be conflicting interests.

This distinctly principle-based conception of fiduciary accountability (i.e., that a general fiduciary principle requiring honourable Crown conduct gives rise to specific fiduciary rules in different contexts) was at the core of Aboriginal law following *Sparrow* and for many years thereafter, and a substantial body of jurisprudence built up around it.[23]

As has been noted, however, in more recent decisions the Supreme Court has been effectively dismantling this fiduciary-based legal frame-

22 *Sparrow, supra* note 1 at 1109.

23 See, generally, J. Timothy S. McCabe, *The Honour of the Crown and its Fiduciary Duties to Aboriginal Peoples* (Markham: LexisNexis Canada, 2008) at 147–232.

work and replacing it with the honour of the Crown-based framework. In *Wewaykum*, for instance, Justice Binnie's decision reads as though he was on a mission to substantially rein in the scope of Crown/Aboriginal fiduciary accountability, starting with this important statement about its jurisdictional boundaries:

> But there are limits. The appellants seemed at times to invoke the "fiduciary duty" as a source of plenary Crown liability covering all aspects of the Crown-Indian band relationship. This overshoots the mark. The fiduciary duty imposed on the Crown does not exist at large but in relation to specific Indian interests. . . .[24]

Further, he states that "not all obligations existing between the parties to a fiduciary relationship are themselves fiduciary in nature,"[25] and he goes on to highlight the inherent conflict of interest that the Crown often finds itself in when tasked with balancing interests between Aboriginal and non-Aboriginal entities, explaining that,

> when exercising ordinary government powers in matters involving disputes between Indians and non-Indians, the Crown was (and is) obliged to have regard to the interest of all affected parties, not just the Indian interest. The Crown can be no ordinary fiduciary; it wears many hats and represents many interests, some of which cannot help but be conflicting. . . . [26]

Binnie J. was clearly uncomfortable with the principle-based fiduciary construct that the Supreme Court had developed for this area to date, and was taking initial steps toward reshaping its fundamentals. However, despite his refrains, Binnie J. still described the content of fiduciary accountability in the circumstances of that case, in an exceedingly principle-based manner, still conceptualizing applicable Crown obligations as flowing from a fiduciary principle.[27]

---

24 *Wewaykum, supra* note 12 at para. 81.

25 *Ibid.* at para. 83.

26 *Ibid.* at paras. 82–83 and 96.

27 *Ibid.* at para. 86.

In *Haida Nation,* however, Chief Justice McLachlin went substantially further than Binnie J. had in *Wewaykum* in terms of dismantling the applicable principle-based fiduciary construct. That is, she instituted a replacement principle (i.e., the honour of the Crown principle) in the place of the previous fiduciary-based principle, and sourced the applicable duty enforced in that case (i.e., the duty to consult and accommodate) to that replacement principle and not to any overarching fiduciary principle, as the British Columbia Court of Appeal had done in that case.

However, despite this doctrinal eclipsing of the previous fiduciary-based construct by the honour of the Crown principle, McLachlin C.J. articulated a delimited, residual jurisdiction for nonconventional fiduciary accountability in Crown/Aboriginal contexts:

> Where the Crown has assumed discretionary control over specific Aboriginal interests, the honour of the Crown gives rise to a fiduciary duty. . . . The content of the fiduciary duty may vary to take into account the Crown's other, broader obligations. However, the duty's fulfilment requires that the Crown act with reference to the Aboriginal group's best interest in exercising discretionary control over the specific Aboriginal interest at stake.[28]

As noted in Chapter Two, this conceptualization of the intersection between Crown honour accountability and Crown fiduciary accountability in Aboriginal contexts fundamentally reversed previous jurisprudence,[29] although this was not acknowledged in the decision.

Against this general backdrop of the key pronouncements in the development of the Supreme Court's nonconventional Crown/Aboriginal fiduciary doctrine, I move now to a more detailed examination of the Supreme Court's jurisprudence in this area.

---

28 *Haida Nation* v. *British Columbia (Minister of Forests),* [2004] 3 S.C.R. 511, 245 D.L.R. (4th) 33 [cited to S.C.R.] at para. 18.

29 In contrast to this conceptualization of Crown honour accountability giving rise to Crown fiduciary accountability, the Supreme Court of Canada had previously interpreted Crown honour accountability as something that was a result of Crown fiduciary accountability: see, e.g., *R.* v. *Van der Peet,* [1996] 2 S.C.R. 507, 137 D.L.R. (4th) 289 at para. 24 [cited to S.C.R.].

a. Function of Crown/Aboriginal fiduciary accountability

Prior to the doctrinal transformation effected in *Haida Nation*, the Supreme Court's *sui generis* and principle-based fiduciary construct constituted the conceptual foundation of Aboriginal law in Canada. In general terms, its function was to regulate Crown conduct in circumstances where there was some potential for adverse impacts to Aboriginal or treaty rights or to *Indian Act*-based reserve land interests that had been tactically surrendered, and to specifically prescribe that in any such instances, the Crown must act honestly, fairly, and honourably in relation to the Aboriginal interests involved. Put another way, the function of Crown/Aboriginal fiduciary accountability was to restrain Crown conduct (or to prohibit applicable Crown dishonour) where deemed necessary to ensure honourable dealings with potentially impacted Aboriginal or treaty rights holders.

At various points, the Supreme Court referred to this function using the language of supervision; that this generalized fiduciary obligation (or ethic) operated to supervise applicable Crown conduct.[30] The effect of this, of course, was that courts could supervise Crown conduct generally.

The doctrinal reordering in *Haida Nation* brought into question the nature of the ongoing function of Crown/Aboriginal fiduciary accountability. That is, the broad functions just described were effectively usurped by the honour of the Crown principle. It is now quite uncertain what function offshoot Crown/Aboriginal fiduciary accountability will serve; it is also quite telling that no function is at all apparent.

As noted, and as we examine in more detail in the next two sections, the prevailing framework (i.e., that set out in *Wewaykum* and *Haida Nation*) dictates that (a) the content of a Crown/Aboriginal fiduciary obligation is to act with reference to the best interests of an Aboriginal community, (b) in a context where the Crown has assumed a sufficient amount of discretion over specific, cognizable interests belonging to that community.

The Supreme Court has not been explicit as to why this type of *sui generis* Crown/Aboriginal fiduciary accountability has been retained as part of the core of Aboriginal law; they have not articulated the general function of this residual type of fiduciary accountability.

The implicit indication from *Haida Nation* and subsequent Supreme Court decisions is that a (still nonconventional) fiduciary duty to act in the

---

30 See, e.g., *Guerin, supra* note 4 at 385; and *Wewaykum, supra* note 12 at 78.

best interests of an Aboriginal community will still apply in circumstances like those which arose in *Guerin*, for instance, where the Crown undertakes a statutory obligation to an Aboriginal community to manage surrendered land interests on their behalf. In such circumstances, the Crown is explicitly tasked with exercising a discretionary power and acting exclusively for the benefit of the First Nation.

So, again, this begs the question: what function (additional to or as some adjunct to those served generally by the over-arching honour of the Crown-based governing framework, and in addition to the explicit statutory mandate that the Crown, effectively, act for the sole benefit of an applicable First Nation) is served by placing a nonconventional fiduciary obligation on the Crown in such circumstances, specifically mandating that it act with reference to the best interests of the Aboriginal community?

It is entirely unclear whether a specific fiduciary obligation, once triggered in such contexts, is intended to function generally to mandate some unarticulated high measure of moral conduct or whether, rather, it is singularly to prohibit a certain type of Crown behaviour (e.g., acting other than exclusively for the benefit of the Aboriginal group). Further clarification from the Supreme Court is required here.

b. Content of Crown/Aboriginal fiduciary duties

Looking at this next incident of the Supreme Court's Crown/Aboriginal fiduciary doctrine — the specific content of Crown/Aboriginal fiduciary accountability — I conceptualize it, again, both prior to and subsequent to the Supreme Court's transformative decision in *Haida Nation*.

Prior to *Haida Nation*, Aboriginal law was structured around a complicated hierarchy of *sui generis* fiduciary principles and obligations. There was a generalized fiduciary principle and specific off-shoot fiduciary obligations. This incident of Crown/Aboriginal fiduciary doctrine is particularly muddled, and takes some work to unpack.

Rotman described this type of construct as a "two-pronged fiduciary duty [owed by the Crown] to Aboriginal peoples," and he explained the dynamics as follows:

> On a macroscopic level, the Crown ought to be understood to owe a general, overarching fiduciary duty to the Aboriginal peoples. . . . In

> addition to the Crown's general duty, the Crown may also owe specific fiduciary duties to particular Aboriginal groups stemming from its particular interactions with them. . . . It is possible for the Crown to owe both a general and one or more specific fiduciary duties to an Aboriginal group as a result of its intercourse with them.[31]

Moreover, a general fiduciary obligation, or principle in the Dworkinian sense, was articulated in *Sparrow* (i.e., a mandate to act honourably) but was seen as a mere extension of *Guerin*. There is an important distinction, however, between the *Sparrow* and *Guerin* conceptualizations of the Crown's respective fiduciary mandate.

In *Guerin*, the Crown's fundamental fiduciary obligation, as stated by Dickson J., was, in effect, to act exclusively for the benefit of the First Nation.[32] Once he observed that obligation to have been triggered, he conceptualized fiduciary doctrine as allowing the Court to then generally (and flexibly) monitor the Crown's conduct in the carrying out of that obligation, as indicated at the outset of this chapter.

In *Sparrow*, however, the fundamental mandate of the fiduciary obligation is described as something distinct from an obligation to act exclusively for the benefit of the First Nation; it is described as a legal mandate to act honourably and with integrity in applicable scenarios. In some instances, it was conceptualized by the Supreme Court as a mandate to merely take into account Aboriginal interests in applicable scenarios.[33] In any event, the fiduciary mandate in *Sparrow* was ultimately, and unequivocally, to involve a balancing of the various Aboriginal and non-Aboriginal interests involved, mindful, of course, of the superior (constitutional) position of interests related to Aboriginal and treaty rights.

This mandate was interpreted by Lambert J. of the British Columbia Court of Appeal in the *Haida Nation* litigation:

> The fiduciary duty of the Crown, federal or provincial, is a duty to behave towards the Indian people with utmost good faith and to put the interests of the Indian people under the protection of the Crown so

31 Rotman, *Fiduciary Law, supra* note 14 at 600–601.

32 *Guerin, supra* note 4 at 387.

33 See, e.g., *R.* v. *Gladstone*, (1996), 137 D.L.R. (4th) 648, [1996] 2 S.C.R. 723 at para. 63 [cited to S.C.R.].

> that, in cases of conflicting rights, the interests of the Indian people, to whom the fiduciary duty is owed, must not be subordinated by the Crown to competing interests of other persons to whom the Crown owes no fiduciary duty.[34]

In effect then, there were two parallel fiduciary constructs within Aboriginal law prior to *Haida Nation*. In the *Guerin* construct, there was both (a) a somewhat generalized fiduciary obligation to act exclusively for the benefit of an Aboriginal community (as it was often interpreted[35]) and, (b) specific fiduciary obligations that could then trigger and vary substantially in form depending on context and, evidently, have little or no connection to the over-arching obligation to act exclusively in the Aboriginal group's interests (i.e., a duty to not act unconscionably, the specific fiduciary duty effectively enforced in *Guerin*, is entirely distinct in substance from a singular obligation to act exclusively in one party's interests).

In the *Sparrow* construct, there was a general fiduciary obligation (or principle) to act with high honour and integrity, and then specific off-shoot fiduciary obligations. The latter, again, were to vary depending on context but, under this construct (unlike in the *Guerin* construct), the off-shoot specific fiduciary obligations were clearly linked to the over-arching general obligation, and played a supporting role in relation thereto. Put another way, a breach of an off-shoot fiduciary obligation under this construct would violate the general principle against Crown dishonour.

So, again, the take away here is that there was a complex hierarchy of fiduciary obligations — inconsistently applied — in Aboriginal law prior to *Haida Nation* involving both general and specific obligations. The general fiduciary obligation described in *Sparrow* which mandated that in applicable scenarios the Crown is to act in accordance with a "high standard of honourable dealing" clearly took the form of a Dworkinian principle which, recall from above, operates to incline a judicial decision one way or another but does not by itself dictate specific results; rather, it may give

34 *Haida Nation* v *British Columbia (Minister of Forests)*, [2002] 2 C.N.L.R. 121, 99 B.C.L.R. (3d) 209 at para. 62 [*Haida Nation BCCA* cited to B.C.L.R.].

35 See, e.g., *Blueberry River Indian Band* v. *Canada (Department of Indian Affairs and Northern Development)*, [1995] 4 S.C.R. 344, [1995] S.C.J. No. 99 (Q.L.) at para. 38 [cited to S.C.R.]; and *Osoyoos Indian Band* v. *Oliver (Town)*, [2001] 3 S.C.R. 746, 206 D.L.R. (4th) 385 at paras. 52 and 53 [cited to S.C.R.].

rise to specific rights and obligations (and rules) in different contexts.[36] Of course, as I noted above, the honour of the Crown principle is of precisely the same varietal.

The threshold fiduciary obligation in *Guerin* (i.e., the obligation to act exclusively for the benefit of a First Nation) does not take the form of a principle. Rather it takes the form of a Dworkinian obligation (or rule); recall that such obligations, by themselves, are capable of adjudicative enforcement as discreet causes of action (unlike principles) and explicitly specify the essential facts necessary to ground liability. Conceptualized accordingly, where the Crown is found in applicable instances not to have acted exclusively in the interests of a First Nation, liability necessarily follows on that basis.

The jurisprudence following *Sparrow* in relation to these doctrinal fundamentals was a conceptual mess. The distinction between the *Guerin* and *Sparrow* constructs, described above, was often missed, and understandably so; that is, despite the description in *Guerin* of the fundamental fiduciary duty as a mandate to act exclusively in the interests of the Aboriginal group, Dickson J. enforced that duty in *Guerin* as though it operated as a more generalized principle that both (a) gave reviewing courts broad, supervisory powers, and (b) could give rise to specific off-shoot Crown obligations (again, once fiduciary accountability was triggered, Dickson J.'s view was that it could then operate to effectively prohibit a broad range of Crown immorality in context).

Furthermore, some courts appeared to understand the *Sparrow* mandate as essentially directing the Crown to act exclusively in the best interests of an Aboriginal community in applicable scenarios,[37] while others interpreted it as intended to be capable of "tolerating conflicts of interest"[38] and fundamentally mandating, more generally, honourable conduct.[39]

Conversely, some courts understood the *Guerin* mandate as generally

36 See Ronald Dworkin, *Taking Rights Seriously* (Cambridge: Harvard University Press, 1977) at 24-35.

37 See, e.g., *Blueberry, supra* note 35 at para. 38.

38 *Mathias* v. *The Queen* (2000), 2001 FCT 480, [2000] F.C.J. No. 1568 (Q.L.) (F.C.T.D.) at para. 473 [*Mathias* cited to FCT] .

39 See, e.g., *Gladstone, supra* note 33 at para. 63; and *Delgamuukw* v. *British Columbia*, [1997] 3 S.C.R. 1010, 153 D.L.R. (4th) 193 at paras. 162 and 190 [cited to S.C.R.].

directing honourable conduct,[40] while others understood it as fundamentally mandating the Crown to act exclusively in the interest of the Aboriginal group.[41] In yet other instances, the two mandate varietals were simply blended together when courts were talking about Crown/Aboriginal fiduciary doctrine, and without explicit acknowledgment of the meaningful distinction between the two.[42]

In any event, and for conceptual context, some examples of specific fiduciary duties explicitly recognized by the Supreme Court in the Crown/Aboriginal context prior to *Haida Nation* include:

- a fiduciary duty to not act unconscionably when exercising statutory discretionary power to manage surrendered First Nation land interests;[43]
- a fiduciary duty to correct errors made in relation to a previous land surrender;[44]
- a fiduciary duty, where the Crown is allotting reserve lands, to secure for the First Nation access to its traditional fishery as part of that allotment;[45] and
- a fiduciary duty to minimally impair a First Nation's interests when the Crown has made a unilateral decision to expropriate reserve lands for public purposes.[46]

In addition, Chief Justice Lamer noted in *Delgamuukw* that in scenarios where the Crown is attempting to justify applicable infringements of Aboriginal or treaty rights, the Crown may, depending on context, owe (a) a

---

40 See, e.g., *Sparrow, supra* note 1 at 1109.

41 See, e.g., *Fairford First Nation* v. *Canada (Attorney General)*, [1999] 2 C.N.L.R. 60, [1998] F.C.J. No. 1632 (Q.L) (F.C.T.D.) at para. 67 ["*Fairford*"].

42 See, e.g., *Mitchell* v. *M.N.R.*, [2001] 1 S.C.R. 911, 2001 SCC 33 at para. 9 [cited to S.C.R.].

43 *Guerin, supra* note 4. Note that in *Wewaykum, supra* note 12 at para. 100, Binnie J. stated that the *Guerin*-begun duty is best conceptualized as a specific duty to "prevent exploitative bargains."

44 *Blueberry, supra* note 35.

45 *R.* v. *Lewis*, [1996] 1 S.C.R. 921, 133 D.L.R. (4th) 700.

46 *Osoyoos, supra* note 35.

fiduciary duty to consult an Aboriginal community regarding a proposed infringement[47] (though, of course, that specific conceptualization was changed in *Haida Nation* and *Mikisew* with the effect that such an obligation now flows from the honour of the Crown principle and not from a fiduciary principle), and/or (b) a fiduciary duty to give Aboriginal interests priority over applicable non-Aboriginal interests regarding a government initiative at issue.[48]

Moving on then, what should now be clear is that the combined effect of *Wewaykum* and *Haida Nation* was a dramatic — and welcome — reorientation of the applicable fundamentals at play here. Certainly, it is evident that the generalized fiduciary obligation (in form, a principle that calls for honourable conduct) has been largely replaced by the honour of the Crown principle which effectively mandates the same thing. It is also evident that off-shoot obligations seen as flowing from the general honour of the Crown principle are (unless explicitly stated) not to be seen as fiduciary in nature (e.g., the duty to consult and accommodate grounded in *Haida Nation* is explicitly a Crown honour-based duty, not some type of *sui generis* fiduciary-based duty).

However, in *Haida Nation*, again, the Supreme Court left explicit jurisdiction for a type of off-shoot specific fiduciary obligation. Regarding the content of such off-shoot fiduciary accountability, recall that Chief Justice McLachlin stated that, while it may vary depending on context, it will fundamentally mandate "that the Crown act with reference to the Aboriginal group's best interest in exercising discretionary control over the specific Aboriginal interest at stake."[49]

This notion that a duty to act in a beneficiary's best interests is itself fiduciary in nature was first indicated in *Guerin*, and then, as we noted in the previous chapter, adopted as part of conventional fiduciary law for a period of time before ultimately being explicitly rejected in *KLB* as doctrinally unsound.[50] That is, a duty to act in the best interest of another is not, conventionally, a fiduciary duty. To the contrary, as noted and as we will consider in

47 *Delgamuukw, supra* note 39 at para. 168.

48 *Ibid.* at para. 162.

49 *Haida Nation, supra* note 28.

50 *K.L.B.* v. *British Columbia*, [2003] 2 S.C.R. 403, 2003 SCC 5 at paras. 44-46 [cited to S.C.R.].

more detail in the next section, an undertaking to act in the best interests of another is an essential precondition to the creation of fiduciary accountability in Canada (i.e., in accordance with the prevailing conventional test),[51] as opposed to being part of the content of any such accountability.

In any event, pursuant to the *Haida Nation* test, this best interests-based duty remains the fundamental type of fiduciary obligation in scenarios where nonconventional Crown/Aboriginal fiduciary accountability is determined to be owing. There are at least three possible ways in which to interpret the content of a mandate to act with reference to the best interests of an Aboriginal beneficiary (i.e., in situations where the Crown has assumed discretionary control over specific interests); that is, three possible ways to conceptualize the content of *Haida Nation*'s nonconventional specific fiduciary obligation construct:

1. as a mandate to bring about the best possible outcome (or a sufficiently positive outcome) for the applicable Aboriginal group;[52]
2. as a mandate to generally act in accordance with a high standard of conduct;[53] or
3. as a singular prohibition against acting other than exclusively for the benefit of the Aboriginal group.[54]

It seems unlikely that the first is either what McLachlin C.J. intended in *Haida Nation* or how the Supreme Court will ultimately develop this nonconventional obligation. Recall that the Chief Justice herself wrote the decision in *KLB* where this type of a mandate was rejected as lacking practical utility, as failing to provide a "workable (legal or justiciable) standard by which to regulate conduct," and as mandating an inappropri-

---

51 For the most recent articulation by the Supreme Court of the prevailing test, see *Elder Advocates, supra* note 5 at para. 36.

52 Of course, this type of results-based analysis (i.e., where a reviewing court has broad after-the-fact supervisory capacity) was, in effect, how the Supreme Court ultimately conceived the mandate generally in cases like *Guerin* and *Wewaykum*.

53 Both *Guerin* and *Sparrow* are capable of being interpreted as mandating this type of generalized fiduciary content.

54 This is how the mandate was generally interpreted in cases like *Blueberry* and *Fairford*.

ate type of result-based analysis.[55]

The second potential interpretation here — as a mandate to generally act in accordance with a high standard of conduct in scenarios that are deemed to trigger fiduciary accountability — also appears unlikely. This would effectively constitute a duplication of (or return to) the fiduciary-based principle that the honour of the Crown construct evidently replaced; a return, that is, to something like the *Wewaykum* mandate (act "with a view to" the best interests of applicable Aboriginal interests, while mindful of conflicts[56]) or the *Gladstone* mandate (act so as to meaningfully "take into account" applicable Aboriginal interests[57]). Furthermore, the fiduciary obligation in this second scenario would not be an obligation (as it is described in *Haida Nation*); rather it would be a principle that gives rise to different types of specific (fiduciary) obligations in context. The nonconventional fiduciary obligation in this scenario would presumably, in effect, operate to take over the role that the honour of the Crown principle would otherwise play (i.e., in those specific circumstances where off-shoot fiduciary accountability is deemed to arise).

This is an unlikely and ill-advised outcome; it would maintain a muddled framework and, as noted in the previous section, there is no apparent function, or practical purpose, for having two different frameworks which essentially mandate the same thing.

It seems most likely, then, that what is intended in terms of the fundamental content of *Haida Nation*-based off-shoot fiduciary duties is that such duties are to prohibit the Crown from acting other than exclusively for the benefit of the Aboriginal group in applicable scenarios, forsaking all other interests (i.e., in accordance with the third above-listed interpretation). The Supreme Court has not been explicit in terms of adopting this interpretation in any of its recent Crown/Aboriginal cases. However, in the relatively recent Supreme Court decision in *Elder Advocates* — which did not involve a Crown/Aboriginal claim but which compelled the Supreme Court to comment at length in its decision on the fundamental nature of Crown/Aboriginal fiduciary accountability — Chief Justice McLachlin said:

---

55 *KLB, supra* note 50 at paras. 44-46.

56 *Wewaykum, supra* note 12 at para. 86.

57 *Gladstone, supra* note 33 at para. 63.

> The government, as a general rule, must act in the interest of all citizens. . . . It is entitled to make distinctions between different groups in the imposition of burdens or provision of benefits. . . . In the Aboriginal context, an exclusive duty in relation to Aboriginal lands is established by the special Crown responsibilities owed to this sector of the population and none other. . . .[58]

Viewing the content of the nonconventional Crown/Aboriginal fiduciary obligation in this manner is, recall from the last chapter, moving somewhat closer to the conventional nature of the content of fiduciary accountability. Conventional fiduciary law prohibits acting in relation to a fiduciary's own interests, whereas this third conceivable account of *Haida Nation*'s fiduciary-based mandate in the Crown/Aboriginal context (i.e., as an effective prohibition against acting other than exclusively in the interests of the applicable Aboriginal group), while certainly prohibiting the Crown from acting in its own interests, would also be potentially focussed on prohibiting the Crown from taking into account the interests of third parties, which is to say that the latter mandate is still capable of prohibiting more than just self-interested Crown conduct.

Again, clarification from the Supreme Court is required here.

c. Contexts in which Crown/Aboriginal fiduciary duties arise

As with the first two incidents of Crown/Aboriginal fiduciary doctrine, I start this section by looking to pre-*Haida Nation* jurisprudence. The focus is on the specific contexts that give rise to fiduciary accountability. Essentially, there were two main types of factual contexts seen, pre-*Haida Nation*, as giving rise to Crown/Aboriginal fiduciary accountability. The first was the *Guerin*-like situation where a First Nation surrenders land interests to the Crown, putting the Crown to a (typically statutory) duty to act as a private agent of sorts in relation to those interests. The second was the *Sparrow*-like situation where the Crown is undertaking a public initiative that has the potential to infringe Aboriginal or treaty rights. In the latter scenario, fiduciary accountability was said to trigger in the form of positive fiduciary obligations to honourably address, and effectively justify, a

58 *Elder Advocates, supra* note 5 at para. 49.

potential rights infringement (i.e., through some combination of methods such as consulting the potentially impacted rights holder, taking steps to minimally impair the Aboriginal interests involved, or giving Aboriginal interests priority over non-Aboriginal interests).[59]

Recall that the *Guerin*-like scenario actually does give rise to conventional fiduciary accountability while the *Sparrow*-like situation does not. That is, the latter involves a particularly novel conception of fiduciary accountability, bearing little if any resemblance to conventional doctrine.

As indicated in the previous section, subsequent Supreme Court jurisprudence at times has misinterpreted the nonconventional *Sparrow* precedent as mandating that fiduciary accountability could arise only in situations where the Crown had undertaken to act exclusively in the best interests of an Aboriginal group or when it would be appropriate to say that they should.[60] In such cases, where the Crown's public law duties to its electorate were seen to conflict with a (claimed) fiduciary duty to act exclusively in the best interest of an Aboriginal group, such a fiduciary duty was seen as precluded.[61]

In other cases, recall, the *Sparrow* precedent was interpreted to the effect that nonconventional Crown/Aboriginal fiduciary obligations could tolerate conflicts of interests; that is, as a generalized and *sui generis* form of fiduciary accountability (i.e., a mandate, essentially, to act honourably) that could arise even in contexts where there were competing interests.[62]

Furthermore, the rhetoric that often accompanied the Supreme Court's description of Crown/Aboriginal fiduciary accountability led many courts[63] and commentators[64] to conclude that it was (or ought to be) a type of at

---

59 This was generally how the *Delgamuukw* Court interpreted *Sparrow*: see *Delgamuukw, supra* note 39 at 162–168.

60 See, e.g., *Blueberry, supra* note 35 at para. 38.

61 See, e.g., *Osoyoos, supra* note 35 at paras. 51–52.

62 See, e.g., *Gladstone, supra* note 33 at para. 63; and *Delgamuukw, supra* note 39 at paras. 162 and 190.

63 See, e.g., *Van der Peet, supra* note 29 at para. 24; *Delgamuukw, supra* note 39 at 162; and *Mitchell, supra* note 42 at para. 9.

64 See, e.g., Leonard Rotman, *Parallel Paths: Fiduciary Doctrine and the Crown-Native Relationship in Canada* (Toronto: University of Toronto Press, 1996) at 11.

large or plenary form of accountability. This fact, however, appears to have led Justice Binnie, in *Wewaykum*, to lament the "flood" of fiduciary duty claims borne from this misperception, and to explicitly reject the notion of a plenary, or over-arching fiduciary principle.[65] After listing a number of different types of claims that had been based on fiduciary duty (i.e., in lower courts),[66] none of which involved facts that would appear to trigger conventional fiduciary accountability, Binnie J. stated:

> I offer no comment about the correctness of the disposition of these particular cases on the facts, none of which are before us for decision, but I think it desirable for the Court to affirm the principle, already mentioned, that not all obligations existing between the parties to a fiduciary relationship are themselves fiduciary in nature (*Lac Minerals, supra,* at p. 597), and that this principle applies to the relationship between the Crown and aboriginal peoples. It is necessary, then, to focus on the particular obligation or interest that is the subject matter of the particular dispute and whether or not the Crown had assumed discretionary control in relation thereto sufficient to ground a fiduciary obligation.[67]

This focus on a requisite threshold in terms of the sufficiency of Crown discretion assumed in relation to specific Aboriginal interests hints at a return to more conventional boundaries for fiduciary accountability in Crown/Aboriginal contexts. Despite his refrain, however, Justice Binnie still acknowledges, in *Wewaykum*, a quite generalized and nonconventional notion of fiduciary accountability arising in two different circumstances where Indian reserve lands are involved — explicitly noting, while doing so, the reality of conflicting non-Aboriginal interests, which conflicting interests, he held, did not preclude a finding of Crown/Aboriginal fiduciary accountability:[68]

1. Circumstances where the Crown is creating reserve lands for a

65 *Wewaykum, supra* note 12 at para. 81.

66 *Ibid.* at para. 82.

67 *Ibid.* at para. 83.

68 *Ibid.* at para. 96.

First Nation (in this context, he articulates the fiduciary duty as essentially mandating honourable conduct, and as a mandate well short of acting exclusively in the interests of the First Nation[69]);

2. Generally, in relation to First Nation reserve lands once created (here he defines the fiduciary duty as prescribing not just honourable dealing generally, but one whose content "expands [i.e., upon reserve creation] to include the protection and preservation of the band's quasi-proprietary interest in the reserve from exploitation."[70])

Two years later, the Supreme Court in *Haida Nation* effectively took Binnie J.'s lament to heart and fundamentally reoriented this area of law. As noted, they installed the honour of the Crown as a replacement principle for the nonconventional fiduciary principle that was, to that point and in its various forms, the core of Aboriginal law.

As for the effective test that now forms part of the Crown honour-based essential legal framework in this area to dictate when fiduciary accountability will trigger, McLachlin C.J., speaking in relation in the circumstances of the *Haida Nation* case, said this:

> Where the Crown has assumed discretionary control over specific Aboriginal interests, the honour of the Crown gives rise to a fiduciary duty. . . . Here, Aboriginal rights and title have been asserted but have not been defined or proven. The Aboriginal interest in question is insufficiently specific for the honour of the Crown to mandate that the Crown act in the Aboriginal group's best interest, as a fiduciary, in

---

69 *Ibid.* at para. 86. It has been argued elsewhere that the fact the fiduciary duty articulated here in *Wewaykum* was in the context of reserve creation in an area outside the traditional territory of the applicable First Nation means the decision is restricted to its facts on that basis, and that reserve creation inside the traditional territory of a First Nation ought to be attended by a stricter (presumably exclusivity based) Crown fiduciary obligation. See Senwung Luk, "Not So Many Hats: The Crown's Fiduciary Obligations to Aboriginal Communities since Guerin" (2013) 76(1) Sask. L. Rev. 1 at 22.

70 *Wewaykum, supra* note 12 at para. 86.

exercising discretionary control over the subject of the right or title.[71]

So, based on the combined *dicta* from *Wewaykum* and *Haida Nation*, we can articulate the current applicable test for when Crown/Aboriginal fiduciary accountability arises as follows: nonconventional Crown/Aboriginal fiduciary accountability will arise when the Crown assumes a sufficient amount of discretion over sufficiently specific Aboriginal interests. The interest in question must be cognizable and the Crown's assumption of discretion over that interest must be such that it "invokes responsibility in the nature of a private law duty."[72]

In terms of the Aboriginal interest that must be the object of the Crown's assumed discretion (i.e., for fiduciary accountability to be said to arise), the explicit indication is that Aboriginal land and land-related interests are the primary but not necessarily explicit focus.[73] We may also note that the interest must be linked to an Aboriginal or treaty right (surrendered First Nation reserve land interests presumably qualify[74]),[75] and that interests based on asserted Aboriginal or treaty rights (i.e., unproven rights) will not suffice.[76]

In terms of what will constitute a measure of discretion (over the specific Aboriginal interests) that is sufficient to ground fiduciary accountability, the Supreme Court was vague in both *Wewaykum* and *Haida Nation*. However, in the recent *Elder Advocates* decision, which involved an unsuccessful attempt to use the Crown/Aboriginal nonconventional conception of fiduciary doctrine in a non-Aboriginal context — a class-action group of elderly patients in long-term care facilities in Alberta were impugning the

71 *Haida Nation, supra* note 28 at para. 18.

72 *Wewaykum, supra* note 12 at para. 85.

73 See, e.g., *Manitoba Métis Federation* v. *Canada (Attorney General)*, 2013 SCC 14, 355 D.L.R. (4th) 577 at para. 51 [cited to S.C.R.]; *Elder Advocates, supra* note 5 at para. 49; and *Ermineskin, supra* note 9 generally.

74 On the question of whether or not a First Nation's quasi-proprietary interest in its reserve lands is fundamentally distinct from Aboriginal title-based interests in land, see, e.g., *Guerin, supra* note 4 at 379-382 and *Osoyoos, supra* note 35 at paras. 41-47, 160-170.

75 *Manitoba Métis Federation, supra* note 73 at para. 53.

76 *Haida Nation, supra* note 28 at para. 18.

Alberta government for an increase in expenses and basing their claim, in part, in Crown fiduciary accountability — McLachlin C.J. spoke to the sufficiency of discretion that would be required for the grounding of such an obligation. Specifically, she stated that "the degree or control exerted by the government over the interest in question must be equivalent or analogous to direct administration of that interest before a fiduciary relationship can be said to arise."[77]

This conceptualization of the sufficiency of assumed Crown discretion is presumably intended to apply in the Crown/Aboriginal context.

Finally, there is one other notable component regarding the *Haida Nation* test for the triggering of fiduciary accountability. That is, the claimed duty must be "in the nature of a private law duty." This component of the framework was rationalized in *Guerin*, and has been confirmed in *post-Haida Nation* decisions as a prevailing component of the current test.[78]

In *Guerin*, Dickson J. held that because the applicable Musqueam's land interest pre-existed Crown sovereignty, that had the effect of making the Crown's duty in administering that interest of a kind that is "in the nature of a private law duty."[79] Specifically, he states:

> the Indians' interest in land is an independent legal interest. It is not a creation of either the legislative or executive branches of government. The Crown's obligation to the Indians with respect to that interest is therefore not a public law duty. While it is not a private law duty in the strict sense either, it is nonetheless in the nature of a private law duty.[80]

Dickson J. appears here to have effectively conceptualized the Crown-Musqueam relationship as something nearing a sovereign-to-sovereign relationship in this context (i.e., in light of the pre-existing nature of the interest), and on that basis held that it was not appropriate to view the Crown's duty as public in nature.[81]

---

77 *Elder Advocates, supra* note 5 at para. 53.

78 *Manitoba Métis Federation, supra* note 73; and *Elder Advocates, supra* note 5.

79 *Guerin, supra* note 4 at 385.

80 *Ibid.*

81 *Ibid.* at 380–385.

This component of the test has questionable utility or appropriateness in the context of the prevailing *Haida Nation*-framed test for Crown/Aboriginal fiduciary accountability. The *Haida Nation* test is more of an essentialist fact-based test than the *Guerin* and *Sparrow* tests, not dissimilar from the prevailing test in conventional fiduciary law. If a scenario arose where the Crown assumed substantial discretion over the land or property interests of an Aboriginal community (to such an extent, for instance, that it constituted direct administration of that interest, falling within the test articulated in *Elder Advocates*), it would seem that applicable fiduciary accountability ought to arise on that basis alone. If the Supreme Court is willing to recognize fiduciary accountability on such facts in non-Aboriginal contexts (as they stated in *Elder Advocates* they would be), then there is no rational basis upon which to deny it in Aboriginal contexts on the basis that the obligation owed is somehow not in the nature of a private law duty. Put another way, there should be no further escape route here for the Crown, and this component of the test should be discarded as redundant.

Moving on, the most recent decision of the Supreme Court to address a claim of fiduciary obligation in a Crown/Aboriginal context was *Manitoba Métis Federation*. The facts of that case were discussed in Chapter Two. The claim of fiduciary accountability in that case was ultimately rejected by the Supreme Court based on (a) the finding that the Métis interest in question was not a "specific or cognizable Aboriginal interest" because it was not linked to a collectively-held Aboriginal or treaty right (meaning it did not meet the nonconventional test from *Haida Nation*) and (b) because there was no evidence that the Crown had undertaken to act exclusively in the interests of the Métis children (meaning it did not meet the conventional test).[82]

The interesting and novel dynamic in *Manitoba Métis Federation*, for present purposes, is the fact that Chief Justice McLachlin stated that Crown fiduciary accountability could arise either in accordance with the *Haida Nation*-based nonconventional test, or the prevailing conventional test articulated most recently in *Elder Advocates*.

This creates a strange and circular dynamic in the Crown/Aboriginal context. That is, in accordance with one of the two operable tests (i.e., the conventional test), a Crown undertaking to act exclusively for the benefit of the Aboriginal group is an essential precondition to a finding of Crown

82 *Manitoba Métis Federation*, *supra* note 73 at paras. 51–64.

fiduciary accountability while, in the other (i.e., the nonconventional test set out in *Wewaykum* and *Haida Nation*), a mandate to act for the benefit of the Aboriginal group is the fundamental content of the fiduciary accountability itself.

As further argued in the next chapter, this aspect of the *Manitoba Métis Federation* decision brings into particularly stark relief just how confused the Supreme Court's Crown/Aboriginal fiduciary doctrine has become, and supports the more general argument that this nonconventional framework is fundamentally structured around judicial reasoning that takes the form of a Dworkinian mistake.

One other Supreme Court decision is noteworthy here. The Court's decision in *Mikisew,* which was decided approximately a year after *Haida Nation*, set out the framework for the application of the duty to consult and accommodate in the context of established treaty rights (i.e., in contrast to *Haida Nation,* which had previously set out the framework for that duty in the context of asserted but unproven rights). In light of the fact that Justice Binnie had held in *Wewaykum* that the Crown may owe both generalized and specific fiduciary duties in circumstances where its conduct may affect a First Nation's reserve lands, there was reason to expect in *Mikisew* — another decision authored by Justice Binnie and in circumstances where the proposed Crown conduct was indeed going to impact the Mikisew's use and enjoyment of its reserve lands[83] — that the duty to consult framework there may have been described as fiduciary-based instead of honour-based. However, that was not the outcome. Addressing the fundamental matter in a somewhat perfunctory manner, Justice Binnie stated only that "the duty to consult is grounded in the honour of the Crown, and it is not necessary for present purposes to invoke fiduciary duties."[84] He made no reference to his *Wewaykum dictum*.

Before moving on to Chapter Five, it is worth reiterating that although the honour of the Crown principle appears to have entirely eclipsed the "general guiding principle" set out in *Sparrow*, which effectively mandates honourable Crown conduct in instances where the Crown is proposing a regulatory initiative with the potential to infringe Aboriginal and treaty rights, the Supreme Court of Canada recently, and regrettably, resorted in

83 *Mikisew Cree First Nation* v. *Canada (Minister of Canadian Heritage)*, [2005] 3 S.C.R. 388, 259 D.L.R. (4th) 610 at para. 51 [cited to S.C.R.].

84 *Ibid.* at para. 51.

two separate decisions[85] to its habit of using fiduciary language when referring to the *Sparrow* justification mandate. Such usage is illogical in the context of the new Crown honour-based framework, and likely to be adjusted in future decisions when the point is directly considered.

85 *Tsilhqot'in Nation* v. *British Columbia*, 2014 SCC 44, [2014] 2 S.C.R. 256 at paras. 80–88 [cited to S.C.R.]; and *Grassy Narrows First Nation* v. *Ontario (Natural Resources)*, 2014 SCC 48, [2014] 2 S.C.R. 447 at para. 50 [cited to S.C.R.].

V

CROWN/ABORIGINAL FIDUCIARY DOCTRINE AS A "MISTAKE"

> The conceptual move across the conventional fiduciary boundary that occurred in *Guerin* was confirmed and further developed in *R. v. Sparrow*. . . . The notion of generally constraining sovereign power through the application of fiduciary responsibility is . . . radical. . . . It has no support or foundation of any kind in the conventional fiduciary jurisprudence. Public power is controlled by fiduciary responsibility, but only to regulate opportunism or corruption.
>
> — Robert Flannigan[1]

AS NOTED AT THE OUTSET, ONE OF MY CENTRAL CONTENTIONS IS THAT THE Supreme Court of Canada's Crown/Aboriginal fiduciary doctrine is structured around a materially flawed core. I have also argued that the Supreme Court has been slowly mending its flawed doctrine, effectively detangling itself from it while, at the same time, ushering in a new construct (i.e., the "essential legal framework" structured around the honour of the Crown principle).

I demonstrated in the last chapter that *Guerin* and *Sparrow*, taken together, incubated a fundamentally nonconventional form of fiduciary accountability. I conceptualized this as a principle-based approach (i.e., structured around the notion that a general fiduciary obligation mandating honourable conduct — actually a Dworkinian principle in form — gives rise to specific, enforceable fiduciary obligations as tailored to context). I explained that this principle-based account is distinct from the conven-

1 "The Boundaries of Fiduciary Accountability" (2004) 83 Can. B. Rev. 35 at 64–65.

tional rule-based approach to fiduciary doctrine, which involves only a singular rule against self-interested conduct.

I also documented the fact that this principle-based approach to fiduciary accountability developed for use in Crown/Aboriginal contexts was, subsequent to *Guerin*, adopted in conventional (non-Aboriginal) contexts and, for a period of time, actually had the effect of shifting the conventional fundamentals of fiduciary law toward this principle-based approach. Finally, I demonstrated how, in recent decisions, the Supreme Court has largely resurrected a rule-based construct for its conventional fiduciary law doctrine, and appears to have jettisoned, or be in the process of jettisoning, the principle-based residue.

My contention in this chapter is that the Supreme Court committed a Dworkinian mistake when they installed a principle-based fiduciary construct at the core of Aboriginal law. To understand Dworkin's concept of judicial mistakes, consider first this brief summary of Dworkin's general account of how judges adjudicate in difficult cases.

Dworkin's rights thesis, as initially set out in *Taking Rights Seriously*[2] and further developed in subsequent works, principally *Law's Empire*,[3] famously analogizes judicial adjudication to a chain novel where each common-law judgement is to be the next best chapter in an ever-expanding legal novel of sorts.[4] In describing the dynamics of the binding nature of legal precedent (i.e., previous chapters in the chain novel), Dworkin explains that in cases where no clear rule is seen to govern a dispute, a judge undertakes a process of creative, but meaningfully constrained, interpretation. To resolve a dispute, the judge must first "take up some view about the novel in progress, some working theory about its characters, plot, genre, theme, and point"[5] (in context, a general political theory in relation to the rights claimed, the institutional character of the political community in which these rights are enjoyed, previous relevant decisions, and the prevailing morality of the community).

2 Ronald Dworkin, *Taking Rights Seriously* (Cambridge: Harvard University Press, 1977).

3 Ronald Dworkin, *Law's Empire* (Cambridge, Mass.: Belknap Press, 1986).

4 See, generally, *ibid.* at 228–232 and 238; and Dworkin, *Taking Rights Seriously*, *supra* note 2 at 81–130.

5 Dworkin, *Law's Empire, supra* note 3 at 230.

The judge is then to search for possible interpretations of the alleged rights and duties in a given dispute that fit the "ulk of the text of the applicable chain novel to date and that could count as the next best chapter, which is for Dworkin the right answer in such cases. Dworkin explains that an eligible interpretation must fit with the earlier chapters (precedents), in the sense that they must count as continuing the novel in progress and not beginning anew.

When more than one possible interpretation generally aligns with the bulk of the text in such cases, the judge is permitted — indeed mandated — to have recourse to "substantive aesthetic judgments, about the importance or insight or realism or beauty of different ideas the novel might be taken to express," and to choose as the superior interpretation, or right answer, that with the most substantive appeal to the novel as a whole. The superior interpretation (i.e., the right answer) among those eligible will be that which has the highest degree of substantive appeal, not to the judge but to the novel as a whole, all things considered.

Dworkin explains that a judge makes a mistake if his or her chapter "leaves unexplained some major structural aspect of the text, a subplot treated as having great dramatic importance or a dominant and repeated metaphor," and that such mistakes are to effectively be disqualified by future judges.[6]

Against this brief sketch of applicable tenets of the Dworkinian account, my argument for the Supreme Court's Crown/Aboriginal fiduciary doctrine constituting a Dworkinian mistake is advanced on two conceptual bases:

1. The technical mistake: the principle-based approach to fiduciary accountability that the Supreme Court created was entirely novel and did not "fit the bulk of the text" (i.e., it was not consistent with applicable precedent, since fiduciary accountability was conventionally a rule-based construct). Moreover, Dickson J. in *Guerin* — and Dickson J. and La Forest J. in *Sparrow* — left entirely unexplained the rule-based fundamentals of the conventional doctrine (i.e., this "major structural aspect of the text, a subplot treated as having great dramatic importance or a dominant and repeated metaphor" was ignored). Put another way,

6 *Ibid.*; and *Taking Rights Seriously*, *supra* note 2 at 118-123.

they used a radically nonconventional interpretation of fiduciary law without acknowledging the nonconventional quality of that usage. On these bases alone, and as detailed further below, the development of the principle-based, nonconventional fiduciary doctrine in the Crown/Aboriginal context fits the description of a Dworkinian mistake.

2. The subjective mistake: even if it could be argued that the Supreme Court's principle-based approach fit enough of the previous text to be seen as an eligible interpretation in *Guerin* and *Sparrow* (which is doubtful, in light of the powerful arguments in support of the technical mistake), there were arguably superior eligible interpretations available to them. One is the interpretation that the Supreme Court eventually articulated in *Haida Nation*, framing Aboriginal law around the honour of the Crown principle instead of Crown fiduciary accountability. Recall that in *Sparrow*, in articulating the general guiding principle that the Crown was always to act in a fiduciary capacity in its dealings with Aboriginal people, Dickson J. and La Forest J. cited the honour of the Crown principle as partial support for that finding.[7] That is to say that the alternate interpretation was right there at their fingertips. The fact that there was more than one eligible interpretation meant that the Court, in each instance, was permitted to have broad recourse to subjective factors in crafting their next best chapter. My contention is that in choosing the fiduciary concept to centrally conceptualize the legal regulation of Crown/Aboriginal relationships in Canada, they took up an interpretation with repugnant implications and, in so doing, arguably committed a second type of Dworkinian mistake.

I comment further on each of these two bases in turn.

The Technical Mistake

The primary technical mistake the Supreme Court made, principally in *Sparrow*, was conceiving fiduciary accountability as capable of operating

7 *R.* v. *Sparrow*, [1990] 1 S.C.R. 1075, 70 D.L.R. (4th) 385 at 1108 [cited to S.C.R.].

as a Dworkinian principle; that is, as capable of legally mandating a generalized form of conduct (i.e., honourable behaviour), enforced through specific, off-shoot obligations tailored to context. As demonstrated in Chapter Three, and mindful of some conflicting precedent to the contrary, it is relatively clear that conventional fiduciary accountability comes in the form of a rule — and not a principle — that seeks to police a singular type of behaviour in a specific type of factual context (i.e., to prohibit self-interested behaviour when one has undertaken to act selflessly in the managing of another's applicable interests). This is to say that conventional fiduciary doctrine follows a rule-based approach. Further, recall that the unique potential for concealed opportunistic behaviour in such contexts is the basis for the blunt, strict relief that developed to attend this type of transgression (i.e., full disgorgement of all profit).

Moreover, in *Guerin*, Dickson J. was evidently of the mistaken view that once a fiduciary obligation triggers, an interpreting judge is then empowered with broad, flexible discretion to monitor the entirety of the exercise of that discretion, instead of singularly, and strictly, mandating that he or she not act in a self-interested manner within the context of the exercise of that discretion. This was the primary "conceptual error" that Flannigan pointed out in his critique of Crown/Aboriginal fiduciary doctrine in 2004, noted at the outset of this book.[8]

Furthermore, a general, fundamental mistake the Supreme Court made in its pre-*Haida Nation* Crown/Aboriginal fiduciary doctrine was interpreting it as capable of mandating one party to act in the best interests of another party. This is not a conventional fiduciary obligation; rather, it was applied in the Crown/Aboriginal context "by assertion rather than analysis."[9] Quite the contrary, and reflecting this mistake, an undertaking to "act in one's best interests" is, as noted in Chapter Three, a requisite precondition for the initial creation of fiduciary accountability, both historically and under the Supreme Court's prevailing conventional test.[10]

Put another way, it is to read conventional doctrine backward to view a

8 Flannigan, "The Boundaries of Fiduciary Accountability," *supra* note 1 at 63.

9 *Breen* v. *Williams*, [1996] HCA 57, (1996) 186 C.L.R. 71 (Aust. H.C.) at 95 [cited to C.L.R.].

10 For the most recent articulation by the Supreme Court of the prevailing test, see *Alberta* v. *Elder Advocates of Alberta Society*, 2011 SCC 24, [2011] 2 S.C.R. 261 at para. 36 [*Elder Advocates* cited to S.C.R.].

mandate to act in the best interests of another as a fiduciary obligation. As explained by Brennan C.J. of the High Court of Australia:

> It would be to stand established principle on its head to reason that because equity considers the defendant to be a fiduciary, therefore the defendant has a legal obligation to act in the interest of the plaintiff so that failure to fulfill that positive obligation represents a breach of fiduciary duty.[11]

As Conaglen explains,

> [while] fiduciaries owe a duty to act in the best interests of their principals, that is not in itself a fiduciary duty. Contrary to the approach taken in some decisions in Canada, Anglo-Australian law contains "no proper foundation for the imposition upon fiduciaries in general of a quasi-tortious duty to act solely in the best interest of their principals."[12]

It was noted above that the Supreme Court struggled to actually apply their principle-based approach consistently. The various types of cases that arose in Crown/Aboriginal contexts post-*Sparrow* forced them to vary the doctrinal fundamentals based on the circumstances of each particular case, thus leaving a demonstrably unresolved jurisprudence and the absence of a clear and workable form of regulation.

As demonstrated in Chapter Four, the Court interpreted the mandate in some instances as a fundamental obligation on the Crown to act exclusively in an applicable Aboriginal group's interests, while in other instances interpreted it as a mandate to honourably incorporate Aboriginal interests in whatever regulatory initiative the Crown was proposing. The latter interpretation clearly contemplates fiduciary accountability owed as part of an exercise of balancing Aboriginal and non-Aboriginal interests, which obviously meant the Crown was not to be prohibited from taking into account conflicting interests (i.e., the interests of third parties or of the elec-

---

11 *Breen* v. *Williams, supra* note 9 at 137-38, cited in Matthew Conaglen, *Fiduciary Loyalty: Protecting the Due Performance of Non-Fiduciary Duties*, (Oxford: Hart Publishing, 2010) at 56.

12 *Fiduciary Loyalty, ibid.* at 57, citing *Breen* v. *Williams, supra* note 9.

torate as a whole) as part of the exercise.

The resulting confusion is unsurprising. It was never made explicit that this nonconventional approach to fiduciary doctrine was to be restricted to the Crown/Aboriginal context. Dickson J. did refer to Crown/Aboriginal fiduciary accountability in *Guerin* as *sui generis*.[13] However, he did not acknowledge (nor is it acknowledged in *Sparrow*) that he was fundamentally altering the doctrinal fundamentals. Although Dickson J. may well have intended his analysis to be confined to the Crown/Aboriginal context, he left much room for misinterpretation on this point; a fact clearly evidenced by subsequent adoption of his analysis in other contexts.

Further, there was no direction on how the conventional approach was to intersect with this new, nonconventional approach. Recall that in neither of the cases that effectively incubated the principle-based approach was judicial authority cited or distinguished, which is to say (again) that the *Guerin* and *Sparrow* Courts left these dynamics entirely unexplained, something that they were not permitted to do in accordance with the Dworkinian account. Subsequent courts, therefore, had no direction on what to do when conventional fiduciary authority was cited in the context of this nonconventional framework (and *vice versa*), and hence the dysfunction and doctrinal paralysis that ensued.

Moreover, Flannigan essentially argued that the nonconventional model here was fundamentally ill-suited for use in the context of generally regulating Crown conduct in Aboriginal law; that fiduciary doctrine is simply not configured to do what was being asked of it. To this end, he stated:

> The main substantive concern with that analytical move is that the fiduciary concept *per se* has no developed capacity to resolve conflict or adjust political claims. Its function is robustly unilateral — to discipline those who exploit their limited access for personal gain.[14]

Finally, and as noted at the outset, while *Haida Nation* effectively (but not explicitly) constitutes the Supreme Court conceding their initial error (i.e., by fundamentally disqualifying Crown fiduciary accountability as the core of Aboriginal law and replacing it with Crown honour accountability),

13 *Guerin* v. *The Queen*, [1984] 2 S.C.R. 335, 13 D.L.R. (4th) 321 at 387 [cited to S.C.R.].

14 Flannigan, "The Boundaries of Fiduciary Accountability," *supra* note 1 at 65.

they so far have explicitly maintained, as part of their new Crown-honour based framework, some ongoing, limited role for the application of a nonconventional Crown/Aboriginal fiduciary obligation.

Flannigan warned that the potential for application of both the conventional and nonconventional approaches to fiduciary doctrine in the Crown/Aboriginal context would prove challenging. He noted specifically that

> certain "fiduciary" obligations of the Crown will be suspended if the Crown is able to satisfy the [*Sparrow*] justification test. Other fiduciary obligations (conventional fiduciary obligations), however, are strict, and no justification will be permitted. That will plainly exacerbate the confusion. In the end, it is unclear how all of this can amount to a tractable regulation.[15]

The Supreme Court's decision in *Manitoba Métis Federation* manifests these dynamics warned of by Flannigan. As noted above, it brings into stark relief the ongoing incongruence in the applicable doctrinal fundamentals; the co-existence of the conventional and nonconventional explicitly directed by Chief Justice McLachlin in that case (i.e., the direction that both the conventional and nonconventional tests can bring about Crown fiduciary accountability in the Aboriginal context) is circular and likely untenable. Again, the Crown mandate to act exclusively in the best interests of an applicable Aboriginal community is the precondition in the conventional test, and the actual fiduciary obligation in the nonconventional.

The Subjective Mistake

Assuming for the moment that the technical mistake was not fatal in accordance with the Dworkinian account (i.e., that the Supreme Court's Crown/Aboriginal fiduciary doctrine is not effectively disqualified on that technical basis alone), we then move to the second part of the analysis, that in which the court was permitted to have recourse to subjective, aesthetic judgements about "the importance or insight or realism or beauty of different ideas the novel might be taken to express." Here the question becomes: was the Supreme Court's choice of the fiduciary concept a good fit for Ab-

15 *Ibid.* at 66.

original law, thinking in terms of the various historical and cross-cultural realities at play in Crown/Aboriginal relationships in Canada? Or might there have been other, preferable eligible interpretations?

Rotman suggested that a virtue of the central use of fiduciary regulation in the context of Crown/Aboriginal relationships is that it provided a "new way of thinking about . . . the [Crown/Aboriginal] relationship."[16] He described fiduciary doctrine as "wonderfully enigmatic" and as having much in the way of untapped potential.[17] I agree with Rotman that the adoption of fiduciary concepts here did provide a new way of conceptualizing Crown/Aboriginal relationships; and indeed reference to Crown/Aboriginal relationships as fundamentally fiduciary in nature became ubiquitous. However, I disagree with there being virtue in that conception.

My personal feeling about the use of fiduciary doctrine to centrally regulate Crown/Aboriginal relationships (i.e., since subjective, aesthetic assessment is precisely the task in the Dworkinian scenario presented) was always unease. As indicated at the outset, one of the disasters of Canada's colonial history is that Crown/Aboriginal relationships have come to resemble a classic fiduciary relationship, one where one party is uniquely at the mercy of the other; where the Crown continues to be in the paternalistic role of protecting Aboriginal peoples from non-Aboriginal peoples (e.g., in accordance with legal frameworks that preclude Aboriginal peoples from deciding to act in their own best interests in dealing with their land and property interests). As noted at the outset, I always felt it constitutionally immoral to bring in a legal framework that could in any way legitimize or reinforce that power imbalance.

Furthermore, in the early years of the development of the Supreme Court's nonconventional Crown/Aboriginal fiduciary doctrine, some leading commentators expressed similar concerns. Professor Patrick Macklem was particularly critical of the Supreme Court's invocation of the fiduciary concept as their central tool for governing Crown conduct in the Aboriginal context, arguing effectively that it would be counterproductive in

---

16 Leonard I. Rotman, "Conceptualizing Crown-Aboriginal Relations," in Law Commission of Canada, *In Whom We Trust: A Forum on Fiduciary Relationships* (Toronto: Irwin Law, 2002) at 26.

17 See, e.g., L. I. Rotman, "Fiduciary Doctrine: A Concept in Need of Understanding," (1996) 34 Alta. L. Rev. 821 at 852.

terms of generally empowering Aboriginal communities.[18] Specifically, he argued that the use of the fiduciary concept here "reproduces [Aboriginal] dependency in a new form" and that it "frustrates rather than facilitates the quest for a greater degree of self-government for Canada's First Nations."[19] He also noted that the use of fiduciary concepts here is evidence of the fact that the Supreme Court is not willing to move away from a "hierarchical" conceptualization of Crown/Aboriginal relationships.[20]

Likewise, Professor Gordon Christie predicted that the use of fiduciary concepts here "may ultimately work against the best interests of Aboriginal peoples."[21] Christie's concern was specifically that the Crown should not be entrusted with discretion to determine what is or is not in the best interests of Aboriginal peoples. He conceptualized "a radical divide between fundamental conceptions of legal interests" as between the Crown and an applicable Aboriginal group (i.e., as what counts as something being in the best interests of that Aboriginal group), and he argued that fact alone "renders the use of fiduciary doctrine hopelessly inappropriate" in the Crown/Aboriginal context.[22]

Moreover, and mindful of the fact that weighing one person's subjective assessment against another's is inherently unscientific (suggesting, for example, that Macklem's, Christie's, or my own subjective interpretation is superior to a given Supreme Court of Canada Justice), evidence that at least one superior "eligible interpretation" was available to both Dickson J. in *Guerin* and Dickson J. and La Forest J. in *Sparrow* thus confirming their initial, chosen interpretations as wrong answers in each instance (recall the "right answer" for Dworkin in such cases is the superior interpreta-

18 Patrick Macklem, "First Nations Self-Government and the Borders of the Canadian Legal Imagination" (1991) 36 McGill L.J.

19 *Ibid.* at 412. For a similar argument, see Mark L. Stevenson and Albert Peeling, "Probing the Parameters of Canada's Crown-Aboriginal Fiduciary Relationship," in Law Commission of Canada, *In Whom We Trust: A Forum on Fiduciary Relationships, supra* note 16 at 7.

20 Macklem, "First Nations Self-Government and the Borders of the Canadian Legal Imagination," *supra* note 18 at 411–412.

21 Gordon Christie, "Considering the Future of the Crown–Aboriginal Relationship," in Law Commission of Canada, *In Whom We Trust: A Forum on Fiduciary Relationships, supra* note 16 at 269.

22 *Ibid.* at 288.

tion), arguably lies in the fact that the Supreme Court has now effectively disqualified their initial interpretation and instead, and as a superior interpretation, installed Crown honour accountability in its place at the core of Canadian Aboriginal law (which was available to them at the time).

It would be helpful, in terms of continuing the project of mending their dysfunctional doctrine, for them to go one step further and explicitly acknowledge their error, and fully jettison — or at least fully theorize — those residual aspects of Aboriginal law that are based on the flawed, non-conventional (principle-based) approach to fiduciary doctrine.

We all make mistakes.

VI

THE NEW FACE OF ABORIGINAL LAW IN CANADA

> . . . a settler people in ongoing encounter with Indigenous peoples must deal honourably with them and, more generally, act in accordance with the virtue of honour. The idea that the honour of the Crown fundamentally characterizes Crown obligations to Aboriginal peoples is important to understand.
>
> — Dwight G. Newman [1]

In previous chapters, my focus has largely been on documenting and critiquing Supreme Court of Canada jurisprudence in Aboriginal law. In this chapter, I change course somewhat to synthesize some of the conclusions drawn in these previous chapters and, ultimately, to comment on what the future appears to hold for judicial regulation of Crown conduct as it relates to Aboriginal and treaty rights.

As indicated, the Supreme Court's jurisprudence has been atypically unclear in this area since Aboriginal and treaty rights were first constitutionally enshrined in 1982. I have argued in this book (a) that this is largely a result of misuse of fiduciary concepts in this area, (b) that, while in recent decisions the Supreme Court has jettisoned some of the more dysfunctional elements of its applicable legal framework, and, specifically, has brought in what appears to be a more functional construct (i.e., the framework based on the honour of the Crown principle), the area remains fundamentally unresolved, and (c) the fact that the fundamentals of Aboriginal law remain unresolved is, to a substantial extent, a result of the fact

1 *Revisiting the Duty to Consult Aboriginal Peoples* (Saskatoon: Purich, 2014) at 27.

that the Supreme Court continues to maintain that some nonconventional types of Crown/Aboriginal fiduciary accountability remain part of the new construct.

Since the shift from a fiduciary-based construct to an honour-based construct has been only partially made, it is not entirely clear where this area of law is heading. What this unfortunately means for potential Aboriginal claimants who feel that the Crown has acted dishonourably in interfering with the exercise of their Aboriginal or treaty rights, is that the law still does not provide sufficient guidance, as it ought to, in terms of telling such claimants what specific obligations the Crown owes them and what a breach of each such obligation typically entails.

In this chapter, then, I begin with a brief synopsis of the central role that the honour of the Crown principle is now configured to play. I then comment on the apparent residual applicability of Crown/Aboriginal fiduciary duties. The role that fiduciary duties are now to play in Crown/Aboriginal contexts remains fundamentally unresolved. That said, I go through several scenarios in an attempt to further demystify and unpack the nature of such duties, and to ultimately comment on how they may be interpreted so as to have functional application moving forward. From there, I look at some of the practical implications of the shift from a fiduciary-based construct to an honour-based construct. Finally, I address the significance of the oft-noted mandate on the Crown to reconcile applicable Crown and Aboriginal interests and comment, specifically, on how this reconciliation mandate conceptually relates to the emergent honour of the Crown-based legal framework (i.e., where it fits in the context of the new construct).

a. Central role of the honour of the Crown principle

Relatively recent clarification from the Supreme Court of Canada confirms that the honour of the Crown principle is a core precept and important anchor for Aboriginal law. It is explicit that the honour of the Crown is a principle and not a rule, and that it is not by itself judicially enforceable (i.e., not a specific cause of action). Rather, it operates, in a doctrinal sense, to give rise to off-shoot Crown obligations such as the now well-developed Crown obligation to consult and accommodate Aboriginal people prior to interfering with the exercise of their Aboriginal or treaty rights. Such off-shoot Crown obligations take rule form and are directly enforceable.

The Supreme Court's previous conceptualization of the foundation of Crown duties in Aboriginal contexts was that section 35 of the *Constitution Act, 1982* implicitly incorporated a fiduciary relationship between the Crown and Aboriginal peoples in Canada, with "the result" that the honour of the Crown was at stake in all Crown/Aboriginal dealings, and effectively that off-shoot Crown obligations could be seen as stemming from the over-arching Crown fiduciary obligation to act honourably. It was never clearly established that the over-arching fiduciary obligation to act honourably was not an enforceable cause of action in its own right. And the Supreme Court's attempts to develop these concepts in isolation from conventional fiduciary doctrine proved ultimately unsuccessful.

This fiduciary-based construct for Aboriginal law was effectively discarded by, taken together, the Supreme Court's decisions in *Wewaykum* and *Haida Nation*. It is now explicit that the honour of the Crown is the plenary principle, and implicit that the fundamental Crown mandate in section 35 is that the Crown is to act, as indicated in the epigraph to this chapter, in accordance with the virtue of honour in all instances where Aboriginal or treaty rights are involved. Put another way, the primary (if not exclusive) function of Aboriginal law, in terms of the specific role of the judiciary, is the regulation of Crown dishonour; it is clear this is the mischief that Aboriginal law seeks to fundamentally prohibit.

To date, there have only been two types of off-shoot Crown obligations explicitly conceived in and since *Haida Nation*. The first, to reiterate, is that the Crown must consult (and, where applicable, accommodate) Aboriginal peoples before initiating conduct that could potentially impact Aboriginal or treaty rights. This duty is becoming quite well developed, having been fleshed out through a series of decisions subsequent to *Haida Nation*.[2]

The second is the one conceived more recently, in *Manitoba Métis Federation*, which holds that the Crown must bring a demonstrably purposive and diligent approach to the discharge of any constitutional obligations it owes to Aboriginal peoples. The nature and scope of this new form of off-shoot Crown obligation is broadly cast and requires substantial fleshing out.

There is also, at least ostensibly, a third type of explicit off-shoot Crown obligation as indicated in *Haida Nation*, which is the Crown/Aboriginal fiduciary duty. In Chapters Four and Five, I examined the nonconventional

---

2 See, generally, *ibid.*

use to which the Supreme Court has put fiduciary doctrine in the Crown/Aboriginal context in Canada, and I ultimately concluded that it has been an ill-conceived doctrinal experiment, and one demonstrably on its last legs. In the next section, I comment on what the future appears to hold for Crown fiduciary duties in Aboriginal contexts (both in the conventional and nonconventional formulations).

Finally, it is worth mentioning here a fourth promontory Crown duty in Aboriginal law that appears destined, along with others, to eventually be adjusted and confirmed as an explicit off-shoot of the honour of the Crown principle instead of a fiduciary-based duty. Recall that in *Sparrow*, the Supreme Court held that whenever the Crown is proposing a regulatory initiative that has the potential to infringe Aboriginal or treaty rights, it has a specific duty to justify such infringement in accordance with the justification test set out in that case. Recall also that this duty to justify was conceptualized in *Sparrow* as stemming from the general guiding principle which, for its part, was defined as stemming from both the honour of the Crown principle and the Crown's applicable fiduciary obligation.[3] Since the honour of the Crown principle has arguably, in effect, eclipsed *Sparrow*'s general guiding principle, it only makes sense in the context of the new framework to understand this duty to justify as an off-shoot of the honour of the Crown principle. The implications of the fact the Supreme Court has continued — unreflectively and for no apparent practical purpose — to use a fiduciary label for this *Sparrow* duty are addressed in the next section.

3 *R.* v. *Sparrow*, [1990] 1 S.C.R. 1075, 70 D.L.R. (4th) 385 at 1108 [cited to S.C.R.].

Table: Conceptualizing the New Face of Aboriginal Law

Anchor principle	**The Honour of the Crown Must be Upheld**
Enforceable, off-shoot Crown honour-based duties	Crown duty to consult and accommodate (*Haida Nation, Mikisew*)
	Crown duty to purposively and diligently fulfill constitutional obligations (*Manitoba Métis Federation*)
	Nonconventional fiduciary duties (to the extent they are not effectively obsolete) *note that important *conventional* fiduciary duties arise in Crown/Aboriginal contexts but not as off-shoots of the honour of the Crown. They arise on their own accord upon certain facts being present.
	Future Crown duties yet to be developed and/or confirmed as honour-based instead of fiduciary-based (categories should never be closed) *Examples:* 1) Crown duty to justify rights infringements (*Sparrow*) 2) Crown duty to give preferential consideration to First Nations when allocating new reserve lands (*Lewis*)

Shifting gears somewhat, the anchor principle for Aboriginal law to the effect that Crown honour must always be upheld in applicable instances bears some similarity to the neighbour principle in tort law. Tort law, of course (sometimes referred to as negligence law), is the area of common law which has developed to generally restrain inter-personal behaviour by specifically regulating against injurious conduct by one member of society against another. In order to conceptualize the new face of Aboriginal law in Canada, it is helpful to undertake a brief comparative analysis to the general structure of tort law.

The manner in which Chief Justice McLachlin incubated the modern version of the honour of the Crown principle in *Haida Nation* is similar to the manner in which Lord Atkin incubated the neighbour principle for tort law in *Donoghue* v. *Stevenson.*[4] In that famous case, a claimant became ill from drinking a beverage that had a partially decomposed snail in it, and which had been purchased in a café. She had no apparent claim against the café owner or the product manufacturer based on any known, enforceable legal obligation. However, Lord Atkin was convinced that her claim was meritorious and literally ruled from the biblical precept that "you are to love your neighbour."[5] And he ultimately gave rise to modern tort law in so doing.

Tort law now follows this general structure: there is an over-arching anchor principle — that we are not to injure our neighbours — and there are off-shoot torts which stem from the neighbour principle. The neighbour principle is not a cause of action in its own right; only specific torts are. Torts develop organically at common law. Each tort is initially conceived in the first case in which it is claimed, and its nature and scope are gradually given form through subsequent decisions. The commission of any tort constitutes an injury and offends the anchor neighbour principle. The central function of tort law is the effective prohibition of injurious conduct, and it is said that it is always possible that new torts may be conceived so long as they develop in general accordance with the accepted doctrinal frameworks of tort law.

Based on early returns, it appears as though *Haida Nation* may well be Aboriginal law's rough equivalent to *Donoghue* v. *Stevenson.* In *Haida Nation*, the Supreme Court was convinced that the Haida Nation had a meri-

4 [1932] A.C. 562.

5 *Ibid.* at 580.

torious claim to the effect that they ought to have been consulted prior to forestry activity taking place on their traditional territory. However, this was in a context where there was no known legal obligation which the Crown could be said to have breached (i.e., since the Haida were taken as having only asserted constitutional rights, but no proven rights).

In upholding the Haida claim, the Supreme Court articulated a new and novel conceptual structure for Aboriginal law which, to a large extent, mirrors the conceptual structure of tort law. There is an over-arching anchor principle — the principle that the Crown must act honourably — and there are off-shoot Crown obligations which stem from the anchor principle. The anchor principle, as indicated, is not a cause of action in its own right; only specific off-shoot Crown obligations are. Off-shoot Crown obligations (such as the duty to consult) develop organically at common law; each is conceived in the first case in which it is claimed and its nature and scope is to be gradually given form through subsequent decisions. The commission of any off-shoot Crown obligation constitutes Crown dishonour and offends the anchor principle. The central function of Aboriginal law is the effective prohibition of Crown dishonour and, presumably, it will always be possible that new types of actionable, off-shoot Crown obligation may be conceived so long as they develop in general accordance with the (still developing) doctrinal frameworks of Aboriginal law.

A significant difference between tort law and Aboriginal law, of course, relates to the fact that the anchor principle in Aboriginal law (and the doctrinal basis upon which off-shoot Crown duties may stem from it) is still very much in its formative years. The fundamentals of tort law, in contrast, are now well enshrined and developed. However, this was not always the case. In Aboriginal law, there is still much fundamental work to be done to arrive at clear and workable frameworks for the effective regulation of Crown dishonour in Aboriginal contexts. But the emergent construct has discernible form, and there is precedent for this precise type of construct, which is encouraging.

b. Limited role for Crown/Aboriginal fiduciary duties

Despite the fact that the honour of the Crown principal has evidently replaced the predecessor fiduciary-labelled principle that the Crown is to act honourably in its dealings with Aboriginal peoples, it is undoubtedly the case that fiduciary accountability, at least in the conventional sense, still has a role to play when it comes to the legal regulation of Crown/Aboriginal relationships.

Recall that in *Haida Nation* the Supreme Court stated that the honour of the Crown principle will in certain instances give rise to specific nonconventional Crown/Aboriginal fiduciary duties owed by the Crown to an Aboriginal community (or communities), and that such duties will fundamentally direct the Crown to act in the best interests of that community in relation to the Aboriginal interests at issue. Recall also that in its recent decisions in *Tsilhqot'in* and *Grassy Narrows*, the Supreme Court — oddly and seemingly unreflectively — continued to use fiduciary language when commenting on Crown obligations that arise as part of *Sparrow*-like justification analyses (i.e., which arise when the Crown is attempting to justify a regulatory decision that may adversely impact Aboriginal or treaty rights). Recall further that in *Manitoba Métis Federation* the Supreme Court directed that fiduciary duties may arise in Crown/Aboriginal contexts either (a) in accordance with the nonconventional *Haida Nation* and *Wewaykum*-framed test, or (b) in accordance with the prevailing, and recently reconfigured, conventional test set out in *Galambos* and *Elder Advocates*. Accordingly, I will consider in this section, in turn, how both conventional and nonconventional fiduciary duties may arise in Crown/Aboriginal contexts moving forward.

Two initial points are noteworthy. First, my primary contention in this section is that there is no longer any practical utility in retaining for Aboriginal law either (a) a nonconventional Crown/Aboriginal fiduciary duty of the kind framed in *Wewaykum* and *Haida Nation*, or (b) a fiduciary label for the distinctly non-fiduciary types of obligations that arise in the context of *Sparrow*-like justification analyses. To the contrary, and as I argue more in the next section, there is demonstrable value in fully and explicitly discarding this residue, leaving space then only for the (important) straightforward application of conventional fiduciary doctrine in Crown/Aboriginal contexts, and the principled development of the new honour of the Crown-based framework.

Second, Crown/Aboriginal fiduciary accountability (of the conventional varietal) arises in a context involving Aboriginal people which is entirely distinct from the types of obligations we are primarily discussing in this chapter. A form of conventional Crown fiduciary accountability is owed to the general electorate with respect to public assets and is, therefore, also (indirectly) owed to Aboriginal peoples in this manner, since Aboriginal peoples are, of course, part of the broader electorate to whom fiduciary accountability is owed. Specifically, both elected and non-elected public officials are regularly entrusted with the discretion to manage public assets and undertake to do so exclusively in the public interest. They owe conventional fiduciary duties to the public to not abuse the power they have been entrusted with by acting in a self-interested manner in relation to the applicable public assets. This type of Crown/Public fiduciary accountability is broadly recognized.[6]

i. Conventional Crown/Aboriginal fiduciary accountability

As indicated, Crown fiduciary duties owed directly to Aboriginal peoples may arise in accordance with the conventional test. Recall from Chapter Three that the conventional test stipulates that fiduciary accountability in Canada now arises where one first undertakes to act exclusively in regard to critical interests of another, having assumed or been assigned a specific discretionary power in relation to the management of those interests such that there is attendant vulnerability in the arrangement. The discretion assumed must be such as to constitute direct administration of the applicable critical interests. Therefore, conventional Crown/Aboriginal fiduciary duties will arise in Crown/Aboriginal contexts when the Crown assumes or is assigned responsibility to directly administer specific interests of an Aboriginal community in circumstances where the Crown has, implicitly or explicitly, undertaken to act exclusively on behalf of that community in relation to those interests.

Conventional fiduciary accountability in such instances will not tolerate conflicts of interests. That is, these are scenarios where the Crown is not permitted to take into account the interests of any third party (including the general electorate) as part of the discharge of the applicable undertaking; to do so would constitute a fiduciary breach. Furthermore, recall that the content of a conventional fiduciary obligation is, essentially, a rule against opportunistic behaviour. Specifically, the prevailing Supreme Court

---

6 See, e.g., Mark Vincent Ellis, *Fiduciary Duties in Canada*, v.2 (Toronto: Thomson Reuters, 2004) at chapter 19; Robert Flannigan, "Fiduciary Control of Political Corruption" (2002) 26 Advocates' Q. 252 at 252; and the Supreme Court of Canada's decision in *Hawrelak* v. *City of Edmonton*, [1976] 1 S.C.R. 387, 54 D.L.R. (3d) 45.

framework states that the rule is one against abuse of power. Regarding the meaning of the term "abuse of power" (or abuse of trust), Chief Justice McLachlin indicated that the primary mischief prohibited by this rule is "promotion of one's own or others' interest at the expense of the beneficiary's interests."[7]

So, with this synopsis of the conventional framework in mind, we can now consider the types of situations that will likely give rise to this conventional type of fiduciary obligation in Crown/Aboriginal contexts in the future. Viewing the various types of situations in which Crown misconduct has been alleged in Aboriginal contexts, two emerge as clear examples of scenarios where conventional fiduciary accountability arises: *Guerin*-like facts (i.e., where the Crown acts on behalf of a First Nation on a specific mandate relating to specific Aboriginal land interests) and *Ermineskin*-like facts (i.e., where the Crown directly manages financial assets of a First Nation).

In each instance: a discretion is assumed by operation of legislation; the assumed discretion relates to critical interests (land in the one instance and money in the other); the nature of the assumed discretion in each instance is such as to constitute direct administration of the interests; and the implicit mandate in each instance is of a kind where the Crown undertakes to act exclusively in the best interest of applicable First Nations in relation to the interests involved.

To be clear, conventional fiduciary accountability arose in the circumstances of both the *Guerin* and *Ermineskin* litigations. That said, in neither case was any apparent breach of a conventional fiduciary obligation committed on the facts. Specifically, and as noted in Chapter Four, it was not really suggested in either case that there had been self-interested conduct on the part of the Crown (e.g., in directly appropriating for itself the value of the entrusted interests or opportunistically diverting the value of the entrusted interests to a third party). There was impugnable conduct, to be sure, but, again, none that took the form of a breach of a conventional fiduciary obligation.

It is a worthwhile exercise, then, to speculate as to what an actual fiduciary breach by the Crown may look like in these types of scenarios. Generally, the conventional fiduciary prohibition in each instance is breached

7 *K.L.B.* v. *British Columbia*, [2003] 2 S.C.R. 403, 2003 SCC 5 at para. 33 [cited to S.C.R.].

where an individual Crown agent or a collective Crown entity puts his or her (or its) self-interest in conflict with the Aboriginal interests it had been entrusted to manage.

In the specific circumstances of *Guerin*, if one of the Crown agents involved in negotiating the land transaction had had a direct, personal, and undisclosed interest in the golf course project (i.e., the use to which the leased Musqueam lands were to be put), that would have constituted a prohibited conflict of interest (i.e., a breach of the conventional fiduciary obligation owed) since that individual would have stood to personally profit from the deal. Further, that Crown agent would have been liable and, in accordance with the potent fiduciary remedy, could have been ordered by a court to fully disgorge to the Musqueam the entirety of the value realized by that Crown actor (and this would be so even in scenarios where the applicable First Nation suffers no financial damages). For its part, the Crown would also, of course, have been vicariously liable for the misconduct of its official in that scenario.

Moreover, if a Crown entity had had an undisclosed interest in the golf course project (e.g., if a Crown corporation owned part of the project and had not disclosed that interest to the Musqueam and obtained the Musqueam's consent to complete the deal despite that conflict), that would also have constituted a classic fiduciary breach and compelled full disgorgement of any profit gained.

In *Ermineskin,* the facts involved a legislative arrangement whereby the Crown had assumed responsibility for managing royalty payments paid to the Ermineskin and Samson First Nations relating to resource activity on reserve lands. The essence of the (unsuccessful) claim was that the Crown had not, over a period of years, invested the royalty money as a prudent investor would have, and that Ermineskin and Samson ought to have been receiving a higher rate of return on their royalties. What should now be clear is that neither (a) conduct such as incompetent or neglectful wealth management services, or (b) a statutory scheme which limits the scope within which the Crown may invest First Nation royalty monies (as was the case in *Ermineskin*), constitutes conduct which may be conceived as a conventional fiduciary breach. It may be tortious or it may well constitute dishonourable Crown conduct (as a breach of some form of Crown duty framed as an off-shoot of the honour of the Crown principle), but it does not constitute a conventional fiduciary breach.

What, then, might an actual breach of a conventional fiduciary duty look like in factual circumstances similar to those that arose in *Ermineskin*? If one of the Crown actors entrusted with managing the Ermineskin and Samson royalties had (a) directly stolen some of those monies, however achieved, or (b) specifically directed some of those monies into an investment in which that Crown actor had an undisclosed personal stake (without the consent of the Ermineskin and/or Samson, and assuming for the moment that the applicable statutory scheme would permit discretionary investment by Crown actors), then both the individual Crown actor and the Crown itself (vicariously) would be liable for a conventional fiduciary breach and may be ordered by a reviewing court to fully disgorge any profit obtained by the Crown or its official.

In sum, conventional fiduciary accountability exists so as to bluntly and singularly dis-incentivize the types of self-interested conduct described in the above hypothetical scenarios. It is a crucially important form of legal obligation on Crown actors despite the fact it is rarely invoked, and its application in Crown/Aboriginal contexts is as crucial as it is anywhere else.

Against this backdrop of how conventional fiduciary accountability is configured to operate in applicable Crown/Aboriginal contexts moving forward, I now consider how nonconventional Crown/Aboriginal fiduciary accountability is configured to operate in parallel with conventional fiduciary accountability in regulating against Crown misconduct (i.e., since parallel regulation by the conventional and the nonconventional was explicitly contemplated in *Manitoba Métis Federation*).

ii. Nonconventional Crown/Aboriginal fiduciary accountability

Recall from the analysis in Chapter Four that there are explicitly two remaining types of nonconventional Crown/Aboriginal fiduciary duties within Aboriginal law, neither of which I believe hold any residual, practical utility. First, and primarily, there is the *Wewaykum* and *Haida Nation*-framed fiduciary duty that entails a prescriptive obligation which, once triggered, mandates the Crown to act with reference to the best interests of an applicable Aboriginal community in circumstances where it has assumed a sufficient amount of discretion over specific Aboriginal interests. The various components of this type of duty were discussed at length in Chapter Four.

The second is the *Sparrow*-framed varietal. Recall that this type of fiduciary accountability is distinct from the *Wewaykum* and *Haida Nation*-

framed fiduciary duties. Here (very nonconventional) Crown fiduciary duties potentially arise in instances where the Crown is contemplating regulatory activity that has the potential to infringe Aboriginal or treaty rights, and is looking to justify such rights infringement as "consistent with the Crown's fiduciary obligation to the [Aboriginal] group."[8] In such cases, the Crown will be able to establish compliance with its applicable fiduciary obligation if it can demonstrate some acceptable combination of (a) having minimally impaired the Aboriginal interests, (b) having prioritized the Aboriginal interest over other interests, and (c) having consulted with the Aboriginal group in question and taken steps to meaningfully address their concerns.

In terms of how each of these two types of nonconventional Crown/Aboriginal fiduciary accountability is likely to apply moving forward, I now address each, in turn.

The *Wewaykum* and *Haida Nation*-framed fiduciary duty

As indicated in Chapter Four, it is unclear how the Crown fiduciary duty articulated in *Wewaykum* and *Haida Nation* is intended to operate. Recall that in *Manitoba Métis Federation,* the Supreme Court stated that fiduciary accountability may arise in either the conventional or nonconventional manner in Crown/Aboriginal contexts. To reiterate, Crown/Aboriginal fiduciary accountably may arise in accordance with either of the following two tests:

1. Conventional: when the Crown assumes responsibility to directly administer specific interests of an Aboriginal community in circumstances where the Crown has, implicitly or explicitly, undertaken to act exclusively in the best interest of that community in relation to those interests; and
2. Nonconventional: when the Crown assumes sufficient discretionary control over sufficiently specific (and cognizable) Aboriginal interests.

These two tests appear to be aligning. The nonconventional test may eas-

8 See, e.g., *Tsilhqot'in Nation* v. *British Columbia*, 2014 SCC 44, [2014] 2 S.C.R. 256 at para. 77 [cited to S.C.R.].

ily be interpreted as synonymous with the conventional. For instance, Binnie J. states vaguely in *Wewaykum* that a Crown fiduciary duty will arise when discretion over Aboriginal interests has been assumed in a manner which is "sufficient to ground a fiduciary obligation."[9] He did not explain what would or would not constitute a sufficient amount of discretion so as to ground the obligation.

However, in the Supreme Court's more recent decision in *Elder Advocates* — which did not involve a Crown/Aboriginal claim but which compelled the Supreme Court to comment at length in its decision on the fundamental nature of Crown/Aboriginal fiduciary accountability — Chief Justice McLachlin stated that an assumed discretion over applicable interests would be sufficient to ground a fiduciary obligation where the applicable arrangement was "equivalent or analogous to direct administration" of those interests.[10]

Presumably, this qualification is intended to apply in Crown/Aboriginal contexts. Furthermore, in most (if not all) instances where the Crown assumes something akin to direct administration over Aboriginal interests, it will arguably be implicit that they are subject to an exclusivity mandate (i.e., to act exclusively in the best interests of the applicable Aboriginal community). Looked at in this manner, the nonconventional and conventional tests are effectively the same.

Whether or not this alignment of the conventional and nonconventional tests for when Crown/Aboriginal fiduciary accountability is in some future instance explicitly acknowledged by the Supreme Court, a particularly acute problem with the prevailing framework arises when we look at the content of Crown/Aboriginal fiduciary duties said to arise in each scenario. To reiterate, the generic content of conventional and nonconventional Crown/Aboriginal fiduciary accountability is as follows:

1. Conventional: a singular prohibition against abuse of power (which is predominantly — if not exclusively — limited to abuses that take the form of self-interested conduct in relation to entrusted interests); and

9 *Wewaykum Indian Band* v. *Canada*, [2002] 4 S.C.R. 245, 220 D.L.R. (4th) 1 at para. 83 [cited to S.C.R.].

10 *Alberta* v. *Elder Advocates of Alberta Society*, 2011 SCC 24, [2011] 2 S.C.R. 261 at para. 53 [cited to S.C.R.].

2. Nonconventional: a positive obligation to act with reference to the best interests of the Aboriginal community involved (relating predominantly — if not exclusively — to Aboriginal lands or land-related interests).

The dysfunction in the prevailing Supreme Court framework is brought into stark relief at this point of the analysis. To be clear, if the conventional and nonconventional tests for when Crown/Aboriginal fiduciary duties arise are effectively the same, as I suggest above, then a clear absurdity results. That is, in effect, (a) Crown/Aboriginal fiduciary accountability would arise where the Crown has undertaken to act exclusively in the best interest of the Aboriginal community involved and then, (b) where the duty does arise, mandate the Crown to act in the best interests of the community. The precondition to the obligation is essentially the same thing as the obligation itself and, as such, the framework is circular and untenable.

If, on the other hand, there remains a meaningful distinction between the conventional and nonconventional tests such that nonconventional Crown/Aboriginal fiduciary accountability may still arise in situations other than those where the Crown has undertaken an exclusivity mandate (so, presumably, in circumstances where the precondition is not the same as the obligation), it is still very difficult to speculate as to how this may all lead to a functional framework. That is, if we persist with the *Manitoba Métis Federation* directive that two different tests are available to potential Aboriginal litigants attempting to frame a claim in Crown/Aboriginal fiduciary accountability (the conventional and the nonconventional), there are still a couple of obvious problems, including:

1. The fact that there remains a circularity issue in that a Crown undertaking to act in the best interests of an Aboriginal community is (a) in the conventional test, the precondition to the obligation arising, and (b) in the nonconventional test, the resultant obligation itself; and
2. The fact that an obligation to act with reference to another's interests is, without confirmation of what this means, a near-meaningless form of obligation.

Recall from Chapter Four that I posited three possible interpretations as to the content of the nonconventional Crown duty to act with reference to the interests of an Aboriginal community and concluded that the only even-nominally compelling interpretation — that is, as something that may potentially serve as a meaningful and functional Crown duty — is that it constitutes a singular exclusivity mandate (i.e., that it effectively functions to prohibit the Crown from acting other than exclusively in furtherance of the Aboriginal interests involved). Recall also that although the Supreme Court has not been explicit on this point in its recent Crown/Aboriginal cases, it is suggested in *Elder Advocates* (again, a case which did not involve an Aboriginal matter) that the nonconventional Crown/Aboriginal fiduciary obligation fundamentally entails an exclusivity mandate.[11]

In what types of specific instances, then, might a nonconventional Crown fiduciary duty — understood as a singular exclusivity mandate — have practical application? What, if anything, does such a duty add to existing mandates? If the duty only arises in *Guerin*-like and *Ermineskin*-like scenarios, then it is relatively clear that it is an entirely redundant form of substantive accountability. An exclusivity mandate already forms part of the legislative mandate in each instance,[12] and the addition of a nonconventional fiduciary duty stipulating precisely the same thing adds nothing from a liability perspective. Although adding nothing in terms of the types of obligations which may be owed in context, the potential that morphing the legislative exclusivity mandate into a fiduciary duty in such instances serves to create more remedial flexibility in instances of breach is discussed in the next section, where I look at practical implications of the shift from the fiduciary-based to the honour-based framework.

If this type of Crown/Aboriginal fiduciary duty to act exclusively in the interests of an Aboriginal community is intended to arise in circumstances other than just *Guerin* and *Ermineskin*-like situations, then the Supreme Court could assist by (a) confirming that this is the case, and (b) identifying the specific types of scenarios where it will arise. Based on post-*Haida Nation* jurisprudence, it is not at all apparent that it is intended to have any broader application. To the contrary, and as has been discussed, the clear

11 *Ibid.* at para. 49.

12 In *Ermineskin*-like scenarios, the exclusivity mandate is largely self-evident and in *Guerin*-like scenarios, it is notable that Dickson J. effectively confirmed in *Guerin* that the legislative duty implicitly entails an exclusivity mandate: *Guerin* v. *The Queen*, [1984] 2 S.C.R. 335, 13 D.L.R. (4th) 321 at 387 [cited to S.C.R.].

indication in cases like *Mikisew* and *Tsilhqot'in*, among others, is that in circumstances where the Crown has some discretion over First Nation reserve lands and Aboriginal title lands (or where the Crown simply retains underlying sovereignty), it is not subject to a general exclusivity mandate regarding such Aboriginal land interests (i.e., the Crown will not be prohibited from adversely impacting First Nation reserve lands or Aboriginal title lands where doing so is deemed necessary in context for the greater public good).

That is, Crown powers in such instances appear destined to be restrained by the promontory "Crown duty to consult and accommodate" (and, where applicable, by the *Sparrow* justification test which, depending on context, may or may not include an explicit requirement for the Crown to seek the consent of the Aboriginal community involved[13]), rather than by a nonconventional fiduciary duty to act exclusively in the interests of an Aboriginal community whose rights may be adversely affected.

Indeed, the predominant debate of late seems focussed not on whether a fiduciary-like exclusivity restraint is operative but, rather, whether or not the consent of adversely-impacted Aboriginal communities ought to be a requisite part of consultation/justification frameworks in certain instances.[14] Put another way, the question is not whether the Crown is under an exclusivity mandate but whether the Crown has any right to unilaterally infringe Aboriginal land interests absent their consent, and if so on what basis.

---

13 See, e.g., *Tsilhqot'in, supra* note 8 at para. 90 where the Supreme Court recently held that where the Aboriginal interest in question relates to an established Aboriginal title right, the Crown will in such scenarios be required to seek the consent of the Aboriginal community prior to undertaking or authorizing infringing activity.

14 The Supreme Court was careful in its wording in *Tsilhqot'in*, indicating that in applicable instances, the Crown will be compelled to seek the consent of the Aboriginal community while also making clear that the Crown may move forward with infringing activity in such instances even if the consent of that Aboriginal community is not successfully obtained: *Tsilhqot'in, supra* note 8 at para. 90. For a perspective on related issues in the international law context, see Mauro Barelli, "Free, Prior and Informed Consent in the Aftermath of the UN Declaration on the Rights of Indigenous Peoples: Developments and Challenges Ahead," (2012) 16 International Journal of Human Rights, 1.

The *Sparrow*-framed fiduciary duty

Moving from the *Wewaykum* and *Haida Nation*-framed to the *Sparrow*-framed varietal of nonconventional fiduciary accountability, recall my contention that the honour of the Crown principle, as articulated in *Haida Nation,* effectively eclipsed this *Sparrow*-type varietal of fiduciary accountability which arises where the Crown is endeavouring to justify an infringement of an Aboriginal or treaty right for some public purpose. Accordingly, it is surprising (and unhelpful) that the Supreme Court chose to continue to use fiduciary language in articulating the *Sparrow* justification test in their recent decisions in both *Tsilhqot'in* and *Grassy Narrows,* thus leading to the — at least temporary — reality that the old *Sparrow*-like type of fiduciary accountability is still technically in play.

To be clear, in using fiduciary language in these recent instances, the Supreme Court is not conceding that the Aboriginal community has full sovereignty, and my contention is that clinging to this residual use of fiduciary language serves no practical utility. Rather, and as I discuss further in the next section, it actually serves to substantially obscure and threaten the future, coherent development of law in this area.

The conceptualization of Crown duties that form part of the *Sparrow* justification test as fiduciary in nature is distinctly nonconventional. Unlike the *Wewaykum* and *Haida Nation*-framed (nonconventional) fiduciary duty — which at least bears ostensible similarity to conventional fiduciary accountability — *Sparrow*-like fiduciary duties bear no conceptual resemblance of any kind to the fiduciary concept. Added to which, the doctrinal foundation upon which these duties were developed (i.e., as part of a construct that effectively framed them as off-shoots of an over-arching fiduciary obligation mandating honourable Crown conduct) was explicitly discarded through *Wewaykum* and *Haida Nation,* where it was confirmed that (a) no such plenary fiduciary obligation exists, and (b) rather, all applicable Crown duties in this area flow from the honour of the Crown principle.

Furthermore, and to break this down a bit further, it is helpful to briefly look at the nature of the specific *Sparrow*-like fiduciary duties that may still conceivably arise in context. That is, and to reiterate, in order to justify an applicable Aboriginal or treaty rights infringement, the Crown must establish that it discharged some combination of the following duties:

1. A fiduciary duty to prioritize Aboriginal interests;
2. A fiduciary duty to minimally impair Aboriginal interests; and/or
3. A fiduciary duty to consult with applicable Aboriginal or treaty rights holders.

Framing these as distinct, positive Crown fiduciary duties is precisely what the Supreme Court did in *Sparrow*, and has consistently done in other decisions since *Sparrow*.

These types of Crown obligations have (a) nothing to do with conventional fiduciary accountability, and (b) everything to do with the upholding of the honour of the Crown. For instance, the Supreme Court has already explicitly stated (in *Haida Nation* and *Mikisew*, respectively) that the third type of fiduciary duty listed above — consultation obligations owed by the Crown to Aboriginal peoples in context — is no longer understood as being fiduciary in nature, but is rather a Crown obligation that stems from the honour of the Crown principle. Likewise, it is an obvious extension of the recent jurisprudence to conclude that the related duties to prioritize and/or to minimally impair Aboriginal interests arise in context as off-shoots of the honour of the Crown principle. Continuing to refer to them as fiduciary in nature serves only to obscure. So again, there is a significant inconsistency in the prevailing framework which, to some extent, obstructs the path toward a coherent and functional framework.

c. Practical implications of replacing the "Crown as fiduciary" concept with the "honour of the Crown" principle

To this point, I have been detailing how the Supreme Court has been replacing its Crown as fiduciary construct with a new framework for Aboriginal law which involves (a) one central principle (i.e., that the Crown must act honourably in its dealings with Aboriginal peoples), and (b) specific, enforceable off-shoot duties. I have also been arguing that the Supreme Court has not yet gone far enough in terms of its project of mending its materially flawed doctrine, and that it ought to fully and finally discard the remaining doctrinal residue insofar as nonconventional fiduciary concepts persist within the new framework. In this section, I comment on the practical implications of the Supreme Court proceeding with this fundamental doctrinal shift.

People may rightly ask: does it matter if off-shoot Crown obligations stem from an honour-based or a fiduciary-based principle, both of which seem to effectively stipulate that the Crown is to act honourably? Does it matter if the Crown's obligation, first enshrined in the *Royal Proclamation, 1763,* to protect and preserve Aboriginal land interests against settler exploitation, is honour-based or fiduciary-based? Is it significant that the Supreme Court held in both *Haida Nation* and *Mikisew* (in the non-treaty and treaty contexts, respectively) that Crown duties to consult and accommodate in relation to Aboriginal interests are honour-based rather than fiduciary-based? My contention is that in each instance — and taken together — it matters a great deal.

As indicated at the outset, there are several reasons to prefer the Crown honour-based framework over a Crown fiduciary-based framework. That said, while there are demonstrable positive implications, there is also a palpable resistance among many (including the Supreme Court of Canada) to bringing the Supreme Court's "Crown as fiduciary" experiment to an explicit end.

I begin here, then, by commenting on what I see as some of the positive implications of the new framework, and then address the apparent nature of the resistance, by some, to it. For illustration purposes, I also point to a type of legislative mechanism (the sections of the *Specific Claims Tribunal Act*[15]), which was developed in the post-*Guerin* context and which explicitly codifies Crown/Aboriginal fiduciary obligations in applicable contexts. Practically, in order to effect the type of change called for in this book (the full discarding of nonconventional Crown/Aboriginal fiduciary obligations), such instances of legislation will also need to be adjusted.

The main benefit of the new framework relates to the need for doctrinal clarity and functionality. As indicated, lower courts (and indeed the Supreme Court of Canada) have struggled for decades to decipher the "lofty and elusive" conceptual foundation of Aboriginal law.[16] Long and expen-

15 R.S.C. 2008, c. 22.

16 For two representative examples (among many), see *Kwakiutl Nation* v. *Canada (Attorney General)* (2006), 152 A.C.W.S. (3d) 552 2006 BCSC 1368 at para. 26; and *Callihoo* v. *Canada (Minister of Indian Affairs and Northern Development)*, 2006 ABQB 1, [2006] 6 W.W.R. 660 at para. 77.

sive litigation over the core nature of this foundation has been common, and has typically resolved little. Many Aboriginal communities have been compelled to expend large amounts of their limited resources in their attempts to hold the Crown accountable for misconduct — but without the benefit of a legal framework that clearly stipulates what obligations the Crown owes them, and what counts as a typical breach of such obligations.

I have argued that the honour of the Crown-based construct is a superior framework for Aboriginal law largely because it is effectively an original idea that can be entirely customized for its intended use in this context (in a manner that properly takes into account the exceedingly complex realities of Crown/Aboriginal relationships in this country). My contention is that the experiment of using the fiduciary concept to fundamentally regulate Crown misconduct in contexts involving Aboriginal peoples failed not only because the Court misconceived the very nature of that concept from the outset, but because the concept was simply not available for fundamental customization in the way that the honour of the Crown principle is.

The Supreme Court attempted to do something entirely novel with the fiduciary concept in Aboriginal law, and they did so without explaining the novel quality of that usage. The common result, as discussed in Chapter Four, was that when subsequent reviewing courts were tasked with enforcing asserted Crown/Aboriginal fiduciary accountability, they were forced to make sense of it in the context not only of the nonconventional Crown/Aboriginal thread of case law that had developed post-*Guerin* but also in the context of centuries-old conventional fiduciary law precedent which, as I demonstrated in Chapter Three, is materially distinct.

Since it is relatively clear that the conventional fiduciary duty involves, singularly, a strict prohibition against self-interested conduct (such conduct constituting, in effect, an impermissible conflict of interest), attempts to apply that prohibition in Crown/Aboriginal interactions — and to apply the *Guerin* and *Sparrow* precedents — proved uniquely awkward and challenging for reviewing courts. As already discussed, there are many reasons for this — including the fact that Aboriginal peoples are in fact part of the Crown and that elected and appointed Crown officials are typically tasked, fundamentally, with balancing conflicting interests — and I need not comment further on that here.

The point for present purposes is that the Supreme Court's case law on Crown/Aboriginal fiduciary accountability ultimately became dysfunctional, with the result that there was no fundamental clarity on the nature of Crown obligations in contexts involving Aboriginal peoples. There was no clarity, that is, on the nature of the restraint to be placed upon the exercise of sovereign Crown power in contexts where such exercise threatened impacts to the constitutional rights of Aboriginal peoples.

Furthermore, reviewing courts struggled mightily to avoid outcomes which they felt would overly restrain Crown powers in such instances, seemingly in fear that direct application of fiduciary concepts might do this. A couple of examples are illustrative. In *Osoyoos*, and in a context where the Crown had expropriated some Osoyoos reserve lands for the purposes of constructing an irrigation canal, the Supreme Court determined that it would be inappropriate to put any fiduciary-like restraint on the applicable Crown decision-making power since, essentially, the Crown must retain ultimate power to exercise necessary public functions. Awkwardly, however, after first denying any fiduciary-based restraint on the Crown's decision-making power, the Court held that only once the expropriation decision had been made, a fiduciary obligation could then arise to moderate how that expropriation would take place so as to ensure that the applicable Osoyoos interest was minimally impaired.[17]

In *Hydro Quebec*,[18] a claim that the National Energy Board, in its capacity as a regulatory decision maker, owed a fiduciary duty to act in the best interests of Aboriginal communities who stood to be adversely impacted by applicable regulatory decisions was denied on the basis, essentially, that the National Energy Board (an agent of the Crown as a creation of Parliament) is a quasi-judicial entity and that its function could not be compromised by a fiduciary-like restraint on its powers to the effect that it had an obligation to act in the best interests of one category of participant (i.e., Aboriginal peoples) in regulatory hearings.

I raise these two examples here for two reasons. First, they help to demonstrate the difficulty that reviewing courts were often faced with in the context of arguments that the Crown owed certain fiduciary obligations to Aboriginal peoples in the exercise of their (administrative, legislative, or judicial) functions. Largely construing the alleged fiduciary obligations as involving a strict duty to act in the best interests of the particular Aborig-

17 *Osoyoos Indian Band* v. *Oliver (Town)*, [2001] 3 S.C.R. 746, 206 D.L.R. (4th) 385 at para. 52 [cited to S.C.R.].

18 *Quebec (Attorney General)* v. *Canada (National Energy Board)*, [1994] 1 S.C.R. 159, 112 D.L.R. (4th) 129.

inal community involved (which, as I have shown, was a misconceptualization of conventional fiduciary accountability), the Supreme Court in each instance denied that any such an obligation existed, with the result that no restraint of any kind was placed on the exercise of Crown decision-making power in either scenario.

Second, it is helpful for present purposes to briefly consider how the outcome may have differed in each case had the claim been based on an off-shoot duty of the honour of the Crown principle (however framed) rather than as a claim based on a breach of a fiduciary obligation. Arguably, the fundamental principle in the Supreme Court's new framework that the Crown must always act honourably in its dealings with Aboriginal peoples should — and is arguably configured to — restrain the exercise of Crown powers in any conceivable instance where such exercise may adversely affect Aboriginal or treaty rights. It should not matter whether the exercise of such power is, for instance, deemed to be in the broader public interest as it was in *Osoyoos*, or whether it is judicial or quasi-judicial in nature as it was in *Hydro Quebec*. What such restraint ought to look like in any instance will vary depending on the circumstances involved, but such restraint should always be there, and there should be no escape routes for the Crown.

In situations like the one that arose in *Osoyoos*, there ought to be a restraint on Crown power at the decision-making stage, with the effect that the Crown should not be able to finalize any decision to adversely impact Aboriginal land interests without first working collaboratively with the Aboriginal community involved to honourably address concerns that may arise as a result of the proposed activity.

Likewise, in situations like the one that arose in *Hydro Quebec*, there ought to be a restraint on Crown powers in the regulatory decision-making context to the effect that the Crown should not be able to authorize activity that could adversely impact Aboriginal interests without first ensuring that the (constitutional) concerns of potentially impacted Aboriginal or treaty rights holders are honourably addressed.

Some initial evidence, then, that the honour of the Crown framework is superior to the fiduciary-based framework for regulating applicable Crown conduct (i.e., from a substantive standpoint — in addition to the obvious benefits of simply having a clear and functional framework) lies in the fact that in both *Osoyoos*-like and *Hydro Quebec*-like scenarios, an enforceable restraint on Crown power has now been established in the post-*Haida Na-*

tion jurisprudence. That is, in *Osoyoos*-like scenarios, Crown powers are now restrained — in accordance, generally, with prevailing case law on the duty to consult and accommodate — both at the decision-making stage and in the manner in which it carries out its applicable undertaking (rather than only the latter being the case, as was true under the old fiduciary-based framework pursuant to *Osoyoos*).

In *Hydro Quebec*-like scenarios, regulatory tribunals may now be taken to owe Crown honour-based obligations directly to Aboriginal communities who appear before them as part of regulatory hearings. Depending on the applicable legislative context, and in area that is still developing,[19] such tribunals may potentially have an obligation (a) to directly consult with potentially impacted Aboriginal or treaty rights holders, and to address any material concerns raised by such rights holders, prior to making applicable regulatory decisions, or (b) to ensure that some other appropriate Crown agency has carried out the requisite consultation and accommodation obligations and to do so, again, prior to making applicable regulatory decisions.[20]

Other examples are at hand, but these two suffice for present purposes. In sum then, as far as positive implications of the new shift are concerned, the new Crown honour-based framework promises what the old Crown as fiduciary construct failed to deliver, which is a functional and coherent legal framework for the regulation of Crown misconduct in relation to Aboriginal and treaty rights. It is crucial that our law makes clear what obligations the Crown owes to Aboriginal peoples and, to date, this has largely not been the case.

I move now to consider the demonstrable resistance among many toward the shift from a fiduciary-based to an honour-based construct.

Several commentators,[21] and indeed the Supreme Court of Canada,

---

19 For general commentary on this point, see Newman, *Revisiting the Duty to Consult Aboriginal Peoples, supra* note 1 at 75–79.

20 *Rio Tinto Alcan Inc.* v. *Carrier Sekani Tribal Council*, 2010 SCC 43, [2010] 2 S.C.R. 650 at paras. 55–58 [cited to S.C.R.].

21 See, e.g., Gordon Christie, "Developing Case Law: The Future of Consultation and Accommodation" (2006) 39 U.B.C. L. Rev. 139; James Reynolds, "The Spectre of Spectra: The Evolution of the Crown's Fiduciary Obligation to Aboriginal Peoples Since *Delgamuukw*," in Maria Morellato, QC, ed., *Aboriginal Law Since Delgamuukw* (Aurora: Canada Law Book, 2009); and Leonard I.

have indicated (explicitly or implicitly) a resistance to discarding the non-conventional fiduciary-based residue from Aboriginal law. That said, and as indicated at the outset, in my research for this book, I was not able to locate any notable substantive commentary for why it may — somehow — be a detrimental development that the Supreme Court is moving away from its Crown as fiduciary construct and eclipsing that construct with the honour of the Crown-based framework (i.e., whether looked at from an Aboriginal viewpoint, or from a settler viewpoint).[22] And the lack of such commentary is telling.

Ultimately, it is not clear why there is such opposition to the shift from Crown fiduciary accountability to the honour of the Crown principle. But one may speculate.

In the years following *Guerin*, the novel use to which the fiduciary concept had been put in that decision was heralded as a positive innovation for Aboriginal law. For instance, in one subjective assessment, the Supreme Court's decision in *Guerin* was ranked "as the tenth most important decision of the Supreme Court of Canada in the twentieth century and among the top thirty significant legal events."[23] I raise this here simply to suggest that people may have an intellectual or emotional attachment to the idea put forth in *Guerin* that the Crown sits in a fiduciary position regarding all the discretion it wields over various Aboriginal interests.

I contend that any hope some may have had that the Supreme Court was going to broadly apply conventional fiduciary obligations in this context was unrealistic. That is, at its conceptual high water mark, strict applica-

---

Rotman, "Wewaykum: A New Spin on the Crown's Fiduciary Obligations to Aboriginal Peoples" (2004) 37 U.B.C. L. Rev. 219.

22 In an isolated instance of a partial argument to this effect, Professor Christie suggested in the immediate aftermath of the release of the Supreme Court's decision in *Haida Nation* that the honour of the Crown principle is a less than "full surrogate" for the overarching Crown/Aboriginal fiduciary obligation and suggested, in perfunctory fashion, that the honour of the Crown principle fundamentally calls for lesser forms of obligation than those that would befall the Crown when seen to be under a nonconventional fiduciary obligation. See Christie, "Developing Case Law: The Future of Consultation and Accommodation," *ibid.* at 159. As has been made clear in this book, Professor Christie's suggestion to this effect is not generally supported by the jurisprudence.

23 Cited in James I. Reynolds, *A Breach of Duty: Fiduciary Obligations and Aboriginal Peoples* (Saskatoon: Purich, 2005) at preface p. x.

tion of conventional fiduciary duties in this context would have effectively stipulated that the Crown is not permitted to act out of self interest in relation to any applicable lands in Canada — whether reserve lands, Aboriginal title lands, or treaty lands to the extent the latter are interpreted as only having been conditionally surrendered to the Crown — even where required for things like roads and power lines, and that any profit obtained by the Crown or by any private entity in relation to any such use of lands (in the past, present, or future) ought to be fully disgorged to applicable Aboriginal communities.

Not only is such an outcome unrealistic from a political standpoint (i.e., just based on the inevitable economic policy arguments against it — and it is not hyperbolic to say that a consequence of such application would have been a bankrupt federation), but is predicated upon a misconceptualization of how conventional fiduciary accountability arises. That is, for the Crown to owe a conventional fiduciary obligation of this kind, the Aboriginal land interest over which the Crown wields discretion must unequivocally and fundamentally belong to the Aboriginal community (the beneficiary) and not to the Crown (the fiduciary). In this instance, however, the Supreme Court made very clear in both *Guerin* and *Sparrow* its position to the effect that underlying sovereignty over all lands in Canada, including Aboriginal lands, effectively belongs to the Crown.

To be clear, I am not in any way suggesting that the Crown's acquisition of sovereignty over the lands that now make up Canada was legitimate nor that it has, through subsequent reconciliation processes, been perfected. That is an unresolved question which I address to some extent in the next section.

My point here is simply that the Supreme Court made clear from the outset — in stating that the Crown holds underlying sovereignty to the lands — that it would not recognize a conventional fiduciary obligation prohibiting the Crown from acting in a self-interested manner in relation to lands and resources in Canada, even where doing so may impact the rights of Aboriginal peoples who have an interest in such lands and resources, proprietary or otherwise. The "self" in this context is the Crown proper which means, collectively, all Canadian citizens (including Aboriginal peoples). As such, Crown entities must, in a sense, act in a self-interested manner — that is their fundamental role.

Accordingly, and for the many reasons espoused to this point in this book, the Supreme Court did a tremendous disservice to Aboriginal peoples by, on the one hand, suggesting (in effect, pretending) that Crown obligations owed to Aboriginal peoples in Canada were fundamentally fiduciary in nature and, on the other hand, in and around the same time, both (a) explicitly rejecting the typical precondition necessary for fiduciary accountability to arise (i.e., that Aboriginal beneficiaries in such arrangements actually own their lands in the form of full sovereignty), and (b) making clear that the remedy that would normally be available for conventional fiduciary breaches — full disgorgement of any profit — would not apply in Crown/Aboriginal contexts. To be clear, the doctrinal chaos that ensued has not served Aboriginal peoples well.

Moreover, the fundamental question of who has rightful sovereignty over Aboriginal lands is as delicate a legal issue as there is in Canada. As indicated, the Supreme Court has been clear that its official position is that underlying sovereignty sits ultimately with the Crown. As I discuss more in the next section, however, the Supreme Court also conceded in *Haida Nation* that Crown sovereignty in at least some areas of Canada is *de facto* only and has not, to date, been rendered entirely legitimate, and further that its legitimacy hinges on the success of a continuing project of meaningful reconciliation of applicable Crown and Aboriginal constitutional interests.[24]

In the context, then, of this resistance to fully jettison Crown/Aboriginal fiduciary accountability (of the nonconventional kind envisioned in *Guerin* and *Sparrow*), it certainly seems conceivable that it stems in part from a desire to hold on to the notion that the use of Crown/Aboriginal fiduciary accountability in this manner helps to reinforce the argument that Aboriginal communities have full sovereignty over their lands.

My contention, however, is that such a desire is misguided. Either Aboriginal communities have full sovereignty over their lands or they do not. If they do (which, of course, is not the current position of the Supreme Court of Canada, even in instances where an Aboriginal community holds established Aboriginal title[25]), then the question of whether or not the Crown can unilaterally, adversely impact such lands (i.e., in the exercise of their public functions) is not one usefully framed as a question of whether or not they owe fiduciary duties. Rather, it is a question of whether or not

---

24 *Haida Nation* v. *British Columbia (Minister of Forests)*, [2004] 3 S.C.R. 511, 245 D.L.R. (4th) 33 at paras. 25 and 32 [cited to S.C.R.].

25 See, e.g., *Tsilhqot'in, supra* note 8.

the Crown has any right to do so. Further, the question ought to be whether or not the Crown requires the consent of an Aboriginal community prior to doing anything that harms the land-related interests of that community.

My contention is that maintaining a form of nonconventional Crown/Aboriginal fiduciary accountability in this area does nothing to further the interests of those (myself included) who would advocate enhanced notions of Aboriginal sovereignty. And to the extent some have advocated use of Crown fiduciary accountability here as part of a well-intentioned instinct toward reinforcing the argument that Aboriginal communities have full sovereignty over their lands, such (unsuccessful) efforts surely failed in part because they constituted attempts to do something indirectly that has not, at least as yet, been achievable directly.

A second potential reason for the reluctance to release nonconventional fiduciary concepts from Aboriginal law, and one alluded to in the previous section, is that doing so may be perceived as having the potential to create a softening of the consequences of Crown misconduct; that is, that the available remedies arising from Crown misconduct may be more limited under a Crown honour-based framework than under a Crown fiduciary-based framework. Recall from Chapter Three that remedies for breaches of conventional fiduciary obligations are the most powerful known to law. A beneficiary need not prove damages and windfalls to a beneficiary are permissible because furtherance of the deterrence objective takes priority. The classic fiduciary remedy is disgorgement to the beneficiary of all profits obtained by the fiduciary.

Simply put, however, the classic fiduciary remedy of disgorgement was never invoked as part of the Supreme Court's use of fiduciary concepts in this area. In the one lone example (*Guerin*) of a Supreme Court decision involving a successful claim by an Aboriginal community based in fiduciary accountability which saw the granting of a substantial financial damages award as against the Crown, principles of equity were utilized in arriving at a more generous award for the Musqueam than would have otherwise been available at law. However, the award granted was not the classic fiduciary remedy of disgorgement of all profits (i.e., it was an equity-based but not a fiduciary-based remedy in the classic sense).

Furthermore, in all other Supreme Court cases in this area where relief was granted, remedies were customized flexibly to the circumstances of the case; none took the specific form of disgorgement and none were otherwise fashioned according to remedial principles reserved for fiduciary breaches.

Importantly, wherever necessary in context to maintain and/or develop flexible remedial precepts for Aboriginal law, the new framework — that built upon the honour of the Crown principle — needs to be, and is initially configured to be, developed accordingly. It is relatively clear that the honour of the Crown is a principle of equity,[26] for instance, meaning that remedies for dishonourable Crown conduct ought arguably to be customized according to the needs of a given situation to ensure that justice be done. Equitable rules in the classic sense, of course, differ from legal rules, and when enforceable transgressions of equitable rules are committed, judges have much more subjective discretion when crafting remedies than is typically the case in instances of a transgression of a legal rule.[27] The Supreme Court could enshrine a *sui generis* remedial principle for this area, for instance, which effectively stipulates that remedies for breaches of Crown dishonour in this area may be crafted according to equitable principles.

It is also important to remember that in instances where the Crown actually commits a conventional fiduciary breach — by putting its own interests, or by an individual Crown agent putting his or her own interests, in conflict with those entrusted interests of an Aboriginal community in scenarios where the Crown has undertaken to act only in the furtherance of the Aboriginal community's interests — it is imperative that the classic fiduciary disgorgement remedy be explicitly available.

There is much work left to be done by the Supreme Court, and remedial rules in this area may (and should) develop in *sui generis* fashion, but there is no apparent reason to fear (from an Aboriginal viewpoint) that the new Crown honour-based framework will lead to any softening of the consequences that are to attend applicable Crown misconduct (frankly, I would posit generally that the Crown has got off relatively lightly in most instances to date where it has been found guilty of misconduct in this area), and

---

26 See, e.g., William Blackstone, *Commentaries on the Laws of England; in Four Books*, Thomas Cooley, ed., (Chicago: Callaghan and Cockraft, 1871) Book 3, c.17 at paras. 254–255, cited in Thomas Isaac, *Aboriginal Law: Commentary and Analysis*, (Saskatoon: Purich, 2012) at 313; and *Mitchell* v. *Peguis Indian Band* (1990), 71 D.L.R. (4th) 193, [1990] 2 S.C.R. 85 where the Supreme Court of Canada relied upon the honour of the Crown principle to craft an equitable remedy.

27 On the nature of equity and equitable remedies, see *Halsbury's Laws of Canada*, 1st Ed., Equitable Remedies (Markham, Ont: LexisNexis Canada, 2012) generally and at HER-1 and HER-5.

no reason to reasonably expect that better remedies would ever have been plausible under the nonconventional fiduciary-based framework.

Finally, it was noted at the outset of this section that if the prescription offered in this book is followed (i.e., that nonconventional Crown/Aboriginal fiduciary concepts are jettisoned from our law), it will be necessary to adjust any legislation that specifically codifies Crown/Aboriginal fiduciary obligations. As one such example, section 14 of the *Specific Claims Tribunal Act* states that First Nations in Canada may file specific claims on, among others, the following bases:

> (c) a breach of a legal obligation arising from the Crown's provision or non-provision of reserve lands, including unilateral undertakings that give rise to a fiduciary obligation at law, or its administration of reserve lands, Indian moneys or other assets of the First Nation
>
> . . .
>
> (f) fraud by employees or agents of the Crown in connection with the acquisition, leasing or disposition of reserve lands.

A couple of observations assist. First, section 14(c) ought to be amended to remove the fiduciary language. An amended section 14(c) could simply include breaches of any legal obligation stemming from the honour of the Crown principle in relation to administration of reserve lands (including provision or non-provision thereof by the Crown), moneys or other applicable First Nation assets.

To be clear, my prescription for removing nonconventional Crown/Aboriginal fiduciary concepts from Aboriginal law means that existing nonconventional Crown/Aboriginal fiduciary obligations (i.e., at common law) are to be reframed as Crown honour-based obligations. So in this context, for instance, the applicable Crown/Aboriginal fiduciary obligations — articulated in cases like *Wewaykum* — to act honourably during the process of reserve creation and to protect and preserve a First Nation's quasi-proprietary interest in reserve lands from exploitation, would be reframed, and in rule-form, as off-shoots of the honour of the Crown principle and as not having any fiduciary quality.

An example of one such duty might be a Crown obligation to give preferential consideration to a First Nation's interests when allocating reserve lands.[28] Such a duty is not fiduciary in nature in the conventional sense and may be cast simply, again, as an off-shoot of the honour of the Crown principle which duty may stand on its own accord as an enforceable cause of action upon breach. This form of duty, then, would qualify under an amended section 14(c) of the *Specific Claims Tribunal Act* in the form I prescribe above.

Second, and as a bit of an aside, section 14(f) of the *Specific Claims Tribunal Act,* set out above, would actually capture a standard type of conventional fiduciary breach articulated in the previous section. That is, in a *Guerin*-like scenario, for instance, where a Crown actor had a personal and undisclosed interest in the golf course project that the Musqueam lands were to be used for, and that actor proceeded with finalizing the lease on behalf of the Musqueam without disclosing that conflict of interest, such conduct would constitute a classic, conventional fiduciary breach and, in effect, a type of fraud contemplated by section 14(f).

d. The significance of the mandate to reconcile Crown and Aboriginal interests

One of the central arguments made in this book is that Aboriginal law in Canada, post-*Haida Nation*, functions primarily if not exclusively to regulate against the mischief of Crown dishonour in circumstances involving Aboriginal and/or treaty rights. Specifically, the role of the judicial branch of government (the Supreme Court of Canada and the lower courts) where it comes to matters in relation to section 35 of the *Constitution Act, 1982* is to adjudicate individual instances where the Crown is alleged to have dishonourably interfered with Aboriginal or treaty rights of Aboriginal

---

28 See, e.g., *R.* v. *Lewis*, [1996] 1 S.C.R. 921, 133 D.L.R. (4th) 700 at paras. 52 and 54 [cited to S.C.R.] where a (fiduciary) duty along these lines was assumed to exist. For an instance where a similarly-framed duty is codified, see section 4.06 of the Saskatchewan Treaty Land Entitlement Framework Agreement which was entered into in 1992 by Canada, Saskatchewan, and several First Nations, and which is given enactment force by the *Saskatchewan Treaty Land Entitlement Act*, R.S.C. 1993, c. 11. The Saskatchewan Treaty Land Entitlement Framework Agreement is available online at the time of publication at: www.saskatchewan.ca/live/first-nations-citizens/lands-and-onsultation/treaty-land-entitlement-framework-agreement.

communities. The judiciary effectively does this through a template process of (a) acknowledging or rejecting alleged Aboriginal or treaty rights in context, and then (b) confirming or rejecting arguments that the Crown has acted dishonourably in some fashion relating to such Aboriginal or treaty rights. Assuming this articulation fairly captures the essence of the new face of Aboriginal law in Canada (at a high level of abstraction), what are we to then make of the oft-noted mandate upon the Crown to fundamentally reconcile Crown and Aboriginal interests? Where does this fit in?

In the first sentence of the Supreme Court's decision in *Mikisew*, Justice Binnie stated that the "fundamental objective of the modern law of aboriginal and treaty rights is the reconciliation of aboriginal peoples and non-aboriginal peoples and their respective claims, interests and ambitions."[29] Similarly, in *Haida Nation*, the Chief Justice talks about the "aim of reconciliation at the heart of Crown-Aboriginal relations," and restates the articulation of the reconciliation mandate first set out in *Delgamuukw*, which states that "the reconciliation of the pre-existence of aboriginal societies with the sovereignty of the Crown" is, effectively, at the heart of Aboriginal law and, specifically, section 35.[30]

Unequivocally, this notion of constitutional Crown/Aboriginal reconciliation is ubiquitous and of fundamental constitutional importance. But how is it supposed to happen? And is it happening? And who is responsible for making sure it happens? And what if it doesn't happen? And will it be an ongoing process or is it intended at some future time to conclude?

This is yet one further example of the lack of clarity in this area. That said, however, and as I have suggested in regard to the honour of the Crown-based framework of specific Crown obligations that has been developing since *Haida Nation*, I contend that overall clarity is emerging and that answers to at least some of these questions are at hand.

To understand, then, the reconciliation mandate and how it fits against the backdrop of the honour of the Crown-based legal construct I have been describing in this book, it is crucial to understand how the fundamental roles differ as between (a) the judicial branch of government, (b) the legislative and executive branches of government, and (c) Aboriginal leaders.

---

29 *Mikisew Cree First Nation* v. *Canada (Minister of Canadian Heritage)*, [2005] 3 S.C.R. 388, 259 D.L.R. (4th) 610 at para. 1 [cited to S.C.R.].

30 *Delgamuukw* v. *British Columbia*, [1997] 3 S.C.R. 1010, 153 D.L.R. (4th) 193 at paras. 14 and 17 [cited to S.C.R.].

In my view, the executive and legislative branches of government, together with Aboriginal leaders, are tasked with collaboratively reconciling interests as part of a very broad policy mandate — or a collective constitutional goal of sorts — of improving Crown/Aboriginal relations and addressing past grievances. The Supreme Court of Canada's account is that this reconciliation process is implicitly mandated by section 35; a conclusion that makes good sense.

A further feature of this constitutional reconciliation dynamic is the explicit concession by the Supreme Court in *Haida Nation* that Crown sovereignty over at least some non-treaty areas in Canada — and, of course, the question of the legitimacy of the extinguishment of Aboriginal land interests in the various historical treaties raises a separate, somewhat unresolved matter of its own accord — has not to date been rendered legitimate.[31] The implication is that unless and until the constitutional reconciliation process reaches some threshold level of success, the legitimacy of Crown sovereignty over applicable Aboriginal lands is in question.

The judiciary, for its part, has no direct role to play in discharging the reconciliation mandate, nor really any direct role in ensuring that it takes place (other than where, for instance, asked to consider making certain constitutional declarations). The judiciary's central role is to effectively police against individual instances of constitutional Crown dishonour. By helping to minimize constitutional Crown dishonour in Aboriginal contexts, the discharge of this judicial role supports and facilitates the broader constitutional reconciliation process, but does not discharge it.

Notably, this conceptualization of the respective roles of the various parties aligns with Dworkin's account of how law works. Dworkin distinguishes "principles" from "policies" and explains that (a) the judiciary principally deals in the former in enforcing (individuated) rights and obligations, while (b) the executive and legislative branches of government principally deal in the latter in promoting broader (non-individuated) community goals and community welfare.[32]

To reiterate, the reconciliation mandate, described in *Haida Nation* as a goal,[33] takes the form of a Dworkinian non-individuated Canadian, consti-

---

31 *Haida Nation, supra* note 24 at paras. 25 and 32.

32 See, e.g., Ronald Dworkin, *Taking Rights Seriously* (Cambridge: Harvard University Press, 1977) at 91 and 111.

33 *Haida Nation, supra* note 24 at para. 35.

tutional policy objective. It is the central policy dictate implicit in section 35 of the *Constitution Act, 1982*. Moreover, in *Haida Nation*, McLachlin C.J. goes to some length to distinguish the reconciliation mandate from the honour of the Crown principle and its off-shoot duties. She states that Crown/Aboriginal reconciliation is "not a final legal remedy in the usual sense"[34] and describes it as an ongoing constitutional process that is best achieved outside the courtroom.[35]

Furthermore, the Chief Justice conceptualizes the mandate of honourable Crown conduct (i.e., enforceable judicially) as serving a protective and facilitative role in relation to the (policy-oriented) reconciliation goal, stating that legally binding the Crown to honourable conduct in particular scenarios regarding alleged (and individuated) rights and obligations is "required if we are to achieve" the strived-for Crown/Aboriginal constitutional reconciliation.[36]

34 *Ibid.* at para. 32.

35 *Ibid.* at para. 38.

36 *Ibid.* at paras. 17, 45, and 49.

VII

CONCLUSION

> This Court has, over time, substituted the principle of the honour of the Crown for a concept — the fiduciary duty — that, in addition to being limited to certain types of relations that did not always concern the constitutional rights of Aboriginal peoples, had paternalistic overtones . . .
>
> — Justice Deschamps in *Little Salmon/Carmacks*[1]

In this book, I have argued that since 1982 the Supreme Court of Canada has failed to make the law as clear as it should be in terms of conceptualizing constitutional-related Crown obligations owed to Aboriginal peoples. This has led to a context where the class of potential Aboriginal claimants — whose Aboriginal and/or treaty rights are adversely impacted by Crown conduct in applicable instances — have no clear direction in terms of efficiently accessing the Canadian legal system for redress. The fundamentals of Aboriginal law have been atypically unclear for decades, and this fact is yet another grievance being endured by Aboriginal peoples in this country.

More hopefully, I have also argued that the relatively new essential legal framework for Aboriginal law, which is fundamentally based on the honour of the Crown principle, holds considerable promise for the project of developing a clear and functional framework for this area. This new framework has discernible boundaries — it has a central principle which singularly prohibits the mischief of Crown dishonour and is enforced through off-shoot obligations that operate to protect against violations of the central prohibition — and appears capable of consistent application and development. There is much work left to be done by the courts in terms of

1 *Beckman* v. *Little Salmon/Carmacks First Nation,* [2010] 3 S.C.R. 103, 326 D.L.R. (4th) at 105 [cited to S.C.R.].

further developing the various components of both the general framework and the applicable off-shoot Crown duties that stem from the honour of the Crown principle. But the seeds of doctrinal clarity have been planted, and there is reason for optimism.

I have posited that by far the most problematic aspect of Aboriginal law, in terms of the ongoing struggle to arrive at clear doctrinal fundamentals, is the lack of clarity as to the intersection between the honour of the Crown principle and the Crown's fiduciary obligations owed to Aboriginal peoples.

I have attempted to isolate both the problem and a proposed solution. In my view, the problem is clear. The Supreme Court's attempted use of nonconventional fiduciary concepts in Aboriginal law failed, and the Supreme Court then sought to address that failure by effectively replacing these nonconventional fiduciary concepts with the honour of the Crown principle. The problem is that it did so by repositioning rather than jettisoning the nonconventional fiduciary concepts within the overall framework, and without acknowledging that this endeavour fundamentally disqualified applicable previous precedent, leaving much confusion and doctrinal overlap.

I have argued that the repositioned nonconventional fiduciary duty in Aboriginal law — as a type of generic off-shoot obligation stemming from the honour of the Crown principle and requiring the Crown to act in the best interests of Aboriginal peoples in applicable contexts — is entirely redundant and of no ongoing practical utility.

The solution, then, is also relatively clear. The Supreme Court can substantially resolve the fundamentals of Aboriginal law by explicitly confirming that fiduciary duties owed by the Crown to Aboriginal peoples in Canada arise only pursuant to the prevailing test in conventional fiduciary law.[2] My modest prescription is that the Supreme Court effectively remove the *sui generis* tag from Crown/Aboriginal fiduciary duties, and confirm there is no ongoing role for any type of nonconventional Crown/Aboriginal fiduciary accountability in Canada. This will necessarily involve an explicit retrenchment of the Supreme Court's direction in *Manitoba Métis Federation* that conventional and nonconventional fiduciary accountability may continue to operate in parallel in the regulation of Crown misconduct

2 For the most recent articulation by the Supreme Court of the prevailing test, see *Alberta* v. *Elder Advocates of Alberta Society*, 2011 SCC 24, [2011] 2 S.C.R. 261 at para. 36 [cited to S.C.R.].

involving Aboriginal peoples (a directive I framed in Chapter Four as circular and untenable). Substantively, nothing will be lost. And this move will put to the side the primary obstacle remaining on the path toward a coherent and functional framework for this area of law.

Conventional Crown/Aboriginal fiduciary obligations will still arise in Crown/Aboriginal contexts to regulate against opportunism and corruption, but only where the Crown has clearly undertaken, by the operation of legislation or otherwise, to act exclusively in the interests of an applicable Aboriginal community — forsaking consideration of any other interest including its own in such undertaking — in relation to specific Aboriginal interests over which the Crown has assumed direct administration. I detailed at some length in section (b)(i) of Chapter Six how the application of conventional fiduciary duties in Crown/Aboriginal contexts may operate moving forward.

I conclude, then, with a return to the eclipse metaphor I invoked at the outset. The Supreme Court has ultimately orchestrated a type of theoretical eclipse in moving the honour of the Crown principle to the core of the regulation of Crown conduct in the Aboriginal context. Early signs of the impending eclipse appeared in cases like *Marshall No. 1* and *Wewaykum* where Justice Binnie began to use the honour of the Crown principle to obscure the (misconceived) nonconventional fiduciary-based legal construct which had been formed principally through *Guerin* and *Sparrow*.

In the language of astronomy, a lunar eclipse is annular when the moon moves in front of the sun but does not completely obscure it. A total eclipse, in contrast, occurs where the moon entirely blocks out the sun. Effectively, a type of annular eclipse occurred in Aboriginal law in cases such as *Marshall No. 1* and *Wewaykum*. Subsequently, the *Haida Nation* and *Manitoba Métis Federation* decisions brought things irresistibly close to a total eclipse. The nonconventional type of fiduciary obligation developed by the Supreme Court in the Crown/Aboriginal context has become nearly imperceptible. And this is a good thing.

INDEX

Aboriginal and treaty rights 42–43, 76–77, 85, 98,
explicit constitutional standing 11–13, 24, 79–80, 114, 148
Crown regulatory powers restrained by 82, 102, 108, 117, 121, 126, 135–37
key decisions in definition of 13, 24–25, 31–36, 101
See also reconciliation of Crown and Aboriginal interests

Aboriginal lands: underlying Crown sovereignty over 139–41, 146

Aboriginal law 23, 148–49
central role of Crown honour principle in 115–20
compared to tort law 120
function of 10
historically 24–25, 78–79, 85, 116
limited role for Crown/Aboriginal fiduciary duties in 120–22
pre-*Haida Nation* 85–89

"abuse of power"/"abuse of trust": regulated by conventional fiduciary law 67–68, 123, 127

Arnot, David 27–28

"best interests" of another party: to act in 10, 16–20, 43–44, 65–66, 69, 84
compared to duty to not act unconscionably 88
duty to act in not fiduciary in nature 66–67, 91–92
in *Haida Nation* 91–93, 125–26
in *Sparrow* 125–26
as precondition in test for fiduciary accountability18, 49, 72, 92, 101, 107, 110, 128
problems with 91–93, 111, 128–29, 149
See also breaches of fiduciary obligations;
conflicts of interest;
self-interested conduct;
test for fiduciary accountability

Binnie J.
in *Little Salmon/Carmacks* 21, 45
in *Marshall No. 1* 33, 150
in *Mikisew* 101, 145
in *Wewaykum* 14, 66–67, 83–84, 96–97, 101, 126–27, 150

breaches of fiduciary obligations 48, 63, 70
conventional 123–25
disgorgement of profits, in context of 58–59, 107, 124–25, 139–42
in *Ermineskin* 124–25
in *Guerin* 124
nonconventional 125–32
nonfiduciary breaches 65–68
softening of consequences of 141–43
See also conflicts of interest;
remedial options;
self-interested conduct

Brennan C.J. 108

Cartwright J. 31

Christie, Gordon 112

Conaglen, Matthew 56–57, 68, 73–74, 108

conflicts of interest 13–14, 19, 44, 63–65, 76–77, 80–84, 108–09, 124, 134, 144
Crown/Aboriginal fiduciary accountability to "tolerate" 14, 89–90, 95, 122
See also "best interests" of another party;
self-interested conduct

Constitution Act, 1982 49
section 35 12, 39, 42, 75, 116, 144, 147

section 37 12
section 52 47

consultation, right of 37–38, 47, 137
See also duty to consult and accommodate

Cromwell J. 52, 67

Crown/Aboriginal fiduciary accountability
content of 86–94
contexts in which arises 94–102
conventional 122–125, 126
function of 85–86
future of 85–86, 123–24
in *Elder Advocates* 127, 129
in *Ermineskin* 77–78, 123, 124–25, 129
in *Guerin* 77–81, 87–90, 95, 124
pre-*Haida Nation* 85–91, 94–97
in *Haida Nation* 20, 76, 84, 88, 92–93, 97–98, 126–31
in *Manitoba Métis Federation* 48-49, 100–01
in *Mikisew* 101
in *Sparrow* 81–82, 87–89, 95, 131–32
in *Wewaykum* 76, 83–84, 96–97, 125, 126–30
nonconventional 51, 125–32
specific duties prior to *Haida Nation* 90–91
Sparrow-framed duty 125–26, 131–32
to "tolerate" conflicts of interest 14, 89–90, 95, 122; *see also* conflicts of interest
triggers for 77, 86–89, 93, 95, 96, 97–98; in the nature of a private law duty as part of triggering test 98–100
Wewaykum and *Haida Nation*-framed duty 125, 126–30
See also "best interests" of other party;
breaches of fiduciary obligations;
test for fiduciary accountability

Crown/Aboriginal nonconventional fiduciary doctrine
as a "mistake" 103–113
in *Guerin* 107
in *Manitoba Métis Federation* 110
in *Sparrow* 106–07, 131–32
principle-based approach 105–06, 113
subjective mistake 106, 110–13
technical mistake 105–10
See also Dworkin

Crown as fiduciary "experiment" 9–10, 15–16, 75,
failure of 11, 18, 59, 93, 114, 117, 133–34, 137
See also replacing Crown as fiduciary concept with honour of the Crown principle

Crown obligations to Aboriginal communities 26, 78–80, 84–90, 111–12, 139–42
fiduciary in nature 9, 12
in *Guerin* 86, 88
prior to *Haida Nation* 17, 27–33, 86
in *Haida Nation* 42–44, 84–90, 100, 121–22
in *Sparrow* 89–90,-130, 131
See also "best interests" of another party;
breaches of fiduciary obligations;
conflicts of interest;
reconciliation;
test for fiduciary accountability

Deschamps J.
in *Little Salmon/Carmacks* 14n23, 45–46, 148

Dickson J.
in *Guerin* 16n26, 64, 71, 77, 80–81, 87, 89, 99–100, 105, 107, 109, 112, 129n12

in *Sparrow* 75, 81–82, 105–07, 109, 112

disgorgement of profits, in context of fiduciary breach 58–59, 107, 124–25, 139–42

dishonour of the Crown 10, 88, 142, 149
- attracting consequences 24
- judiciary's role in 22, 144–45, 146
- legally actionable in Canada 25, 38, 63, 116, 120, 144–45
- in respect to treatment of Aboriginal peoples 35, 78–79, 85, 115, 120, 144–45

duty to consult and accommodate 10, 37–40, 45, 51, 115–16, 118, 130, 132–33, 137
- in *Haida Nation* 38–42, 47, 85, 91, 119
- in *Mikisew* 101

duty to give preferential consideration to First Nations when allocating new reserve lands 90n42, 118

duty to justify rights infringements 117, 118, 121
- in *Sparrow* 39, 82, 95, 102, 110, 117, 130–31

duty to not act unconscionably 88

duty to purposively and diligently fulfill constitutional obligations 10, 45, 47–51, 116, 118

Dworkin, Ronald 20, 22–23
- "mistakes" 20, 81, 101, 104–07, 110
- principles 22-23, 56, 87, 89, 103, 107, 112, 146–47
- rights thesis 104
- rules 22-23, 56

"experiment"; *see* Crown as fiduciary "experiment"

express trusts 69, 80

fiduciary accountability; *see* fiduciary law
- *See also* breaches of fiduciary obligations;
- Crown obligations to Aboriginal communities;
- test for fiduciary accountability

fiduciary law: conventional
- "abuse of power"/"abuse of trust" regulated in 67–68, 123, 127
- to act in another's "best interests"; *see* "best interests" of another party
- content of 62–68, 76, 83–84
- contexts in which arises 68–74, 123–25
- described 54–57, 62
- function(s) of 60–62
- ill-defined 52–53, 59–60
- nature of based on a "conceptual error" 14, 61, 73–74, 81, 103, 107
- principle based 105–06, 113
- vs. rule based 56–57, 59–68, 75, 78, 82–85
- remedies in 57–59, 129, 141–43; *see also* disgorgement of profits
- strictness of 57–59
- *See also* breaches of fiduciary obligations;
- conflicts of interest;
- test for fiduciary accountability

fiduciary law: nonconventional application in Crown/Aboriginal contexts 17, 75–102, 109; *see also* Crown/Aboriginal fiduciary accountability
- *sui generis* nature of 76, 81, 85–86, 95, 109
- *See also* breaches of fiduciary obligations

fiduciary relationships, defined 9, 69
- vs. fiduciary obligations 52–53

fiduciary role of Crown 13–14

as "experiment"; *see* Crown as fiduciary "experiment"
in *Guerin* 34–35, 53–54
in *Haida Nation* 43
in *Hydro Quebec* 135–37
in *Manitoba Métis Federation* 48
in *Osoyoos* 135–37
in *Sparrow* 53, 81–82
nexus with honour of the Crown principle 36, 43–45, 47, 75, 109, 149
resistance to honour of the Crown principle as replacing 21–22, 51, 133, 137–41

Flannigan, Robert 14, 54n10, 56–57, 61, 109–10
fiduciary doctrine based on a "conceptual error" 14, 73–74, 81, 103, 107

Gwynne J. 31

Halfyard J. in *Haida Nation* 39–41

honour of the Crown
application in modern as well as historical treaties 46, 49–50
as compelling a relaxing of procedural defenses 46–47
as core precept 25–26, 42–43, 45, 115
as supplying deficiencies to treaties 33, 46
central role of in Aboriginal law 115–20
compared to neighbor principle in tort law 119–120
enforceable restraint 136–37
in pre-*Haida Nation* 27–30, 34–37, 85–91
in *Haida Nation* 15, 19, 25–26, 37–44, 51, 84, 97–98, 91, 119–21
post *Haida Nation* 44–51, 91
historic roots of 27–33, 116
in *Sparrow* 34–37, 87, 102
nexus with fiduciary role of Crown 36, 43–45, 47, 75, 109, 149
not a cause of action 46, 115, 120
resistance to honour of the Crown principle as replacing Crown as fiduciary 21–22, 51, 133, 137–41
See also offshoot Crown legal obligations;
replacing Crown as fiduciary with honour of the Crown principle

Indian Act 29, 31, 34, 78–79, 85

La Forest J. 16, 71, 73, 75n3
in *Lac Minerals* 53n4, 64–65,
in *Sparrow* 75, 105–06, 112

Lambert J.A. in *Haida Nation* 41–42, 87–88

Lamer C.J.
in *Delgamuukw* 40, 42, 91
in *Van der Peet* 37, 43

Laskin J. in *Can. Aero* 63–64

MacKinnon A.C.J.O in *Taylor and Williams* 25, 32

Macklem, Patrick 111–12

Manitoba Act 47–48

McEachern C.J.B.C. in *Critchley* 59, 70

McLachlin C.J.
in *Elder Advocates* 67–68, 72, 94, 99, 100–01, 127
in *Haida Nation* 25–26, 37, 42–44, 84, 91, 93, 97, 119, 147
in *Hodgkinson* 72, 93,
in *KLB* 65–66, 67–68, 123
in *Manitoba Métis Federation* 110
in *Mitchell* 43

Millet L.J. 67

mistake; *see* Crown/Aboriginal non-conventional fiduciary doctrine as a mistake

National Energy Board 135

negligence law 119

neighbour principle 119

offshoot Crown legal obligations 115–17, 120, 133, 147, 148–49
duty to not act unconscionably 88
enforceable 10, 25, 41, 46, 47, 84, 107, 132, 136–37
explicitly identified 10, 47, 49, 51, 88, 91, 116–17
future of 85–86, 93, 116, 143–44
in and post *Haida Nation* 25, 43–45, 47, 85, 91, 116–17, 136–37, 147
in *Manitoba Métis Federation* 48–49, 116
See also duty to consult and accommodate; duty to give preferential consideration to First Nations when allocating new reserve lands; duty to justify; duty to purposively and diligently fulfill constitutional obligations

power/trust: abuse of regulated by conventional fiduciary law 67–68, 123, 127
in the nature of a private law duty: part of triggering test for fiduciary accountability 98–100

public law duty 95, 99–100

Rand J. 62–63

reconciliation of Crown and Aboriginal interests 22, 49, 77, 115, 139–40
mandate to 144–47

regulatory powers of the Crown restrained by Aboriginal and treaty rights, 82, 102, 108, 117, 121, 126, 135–37

remedial options 140–43
against fiduciary breach 57–59, 129, 140, 141–43
disgorgement of profits, in context of fiduciary breach 58–59, 107, 124–25, 139–42
in *Guerin* 124, 141

replacing Crown as fiduciary concept with honour of the Crown principle 14–15, 21–22, 45, 83–85, 91, 93, 97, 109–10, 115, 120–21
practical implications of 129, 132–37
resistance to 21–22, 51, 133, 137–41

resistance to honour of the Crown principle as replacing Crown as fiduciary concept 21–22, 51, 133, 137–41

Rothstein J. in *Manitoba Métis Federation* 50–51

Rotman, Leonard 36n42, 56–57, 61–62, 87–88, 111

Royal Proclamation (1763) 41, 46, 78–79, 133

self-interested conduct
disgorgement of profits, in context of breach 58–59, 107, 124–25, 139–42
remedies against 57–59, 129, 141–43
strict prohibition against 23, 57–64, 69, 92, 107, 122, 134, 150
See also "best interests of another party; conflict of interest

Specific Claims Tribunal Act 143, 144

sui generis nature of Crown/Aboriginal context 76, 81, 85–86, 95, 109

test for fiduciary accountability 58, 70–74, 77, 97–99, 107–08, 121, 131, 149
preconditions for 18, 49, 72, 92, 101, 107, 110, 128
conventional and nonconventional 122, 127–29
legitimate expectations test 71–73
power-ceding test 72

in the nature of a private law duty 98–100
test in *Elder Advocates* 19n33, 72, 94, 98n73, 99–101, 121, 127, 129
test in *Frame* 71–72
test in *Guerin* 70–71, 77, 80, 91, 99–100
test in *Haida Nation* 85–86, 92–93, 99–101, 121
test in *Manitoba Métis Federation* 48, 100–01, 110, 128
test in *Sparrow* 39, 82, 89–90, 99, 110, 117, 131, 130–32
test in *Wewaykum* 93, 96–98, 101, 121, 125, 126–30

tort law 119–120

treaties: honour of the Crown in context of 30–31, 33, 46,
modern vs. historical 46, 49–50, 146

trust/power: abuse of regulated by conventional fiduciary law 67–68, 123, 127

unconscionability, in *Guerin* 80–81, 88, 90

Weinrib, Ernest 73

Wilson J. in *Frame* 71–72, 80

CASES

Alberta v. *Elder Advocates of Alberta Society*
test for fiduciary accountability 19n33, 72, 94, 98n73, 99–101, 121, 127, 129
on abuse of power 67–68

Beckman v. *Little Salmon/Carmacks First Nation* 15n23, 21, 45–46

Blueberry River Indian Band v. *Canada (Department of Indian Affairs and Northern Development)*, 92n54, 95n60

C.A. v. *Critchley* 59, 70

Calder et al. v. *Attorney-General of British Columbia* 11–12, 30, 37

Delgamuukw v. *British Columbia* 13, 37, 40, 91, 95n59, 145

Ermineskin Indian Band and Nation v. *Canada* 77–78, 123, 124–25, 129

Fairford First Nation v. *Canada (Attorney General)* 92n54

Frame v. *Smith* 71–72

Galambos v. *Perez* 67, 72, 121

Grassy Narrows First Nation v. *Ontario (Natural Resources)* 11, 121, 131

Guerin v. *The Queen* 9, 13, 20, 64, 77–81
fiduciary concepts in 78–81, 89
Crown/Aboriginal fiduciary principle 14, 34, 52–55, 64, 71, 78–79, 87, 88
test for fiduciary accountability 70–71, 77, 80, 91, 99–100
"unconscionability" 80–81, 88, 90

Haida Nation v. *British Columbia (Minister of Forests)* 9–11, 20, 97, 132
background 38–39
best interests principle 91–93, 125–26
discarding nonconventional fiduciary-based principle 14–15, 36, 51, 91, 109–10
honour of the Crown principle 15, 19, 25–26, 37–44, 51, 84, 91, 119–21
off-shoot Crown legal obligations 10, 85, 91, 116
reconciliation 145–47
test for fiduciary accountability 18, 85–86, 92–93, 99–101, 121
BC Court of Appeal 41–42
BC Supreme Court 39–41
Supreme Court of Canada 42–44

Hodgkinson v. *Simms* 58–59notes

K.L.B. v. *British Columbia* 65–67, 92, 93

Lac Minerals Ltd. v. *International Corona Resources Ltd.* 64, 69

Manitoba Metis Federation v. *Canada (Attorney General)* 10, 18, 45, 47–51
fiduciary obligation in 100–01, 116, 121
leading to conventional and non-conventional fiduciary accountability in Aboriginal law 21, 110, 125, 126, 149
test for fiduciary accountability 48, 100–01, 110, 128

McInerney v. *MacDonald* 65

Mikisew Cree First Nation v. *Canada (Minister of Canadian Heritage)* 129–30, 145
duty to consult 10n4, 37, 91, 101, 132, 133,
Mitchell v. *M.N.R.* 26n13, 43

Mitchell v. *Peguis Indian Band* 29n24, 142n26

Osoyoos Indian Band v. *Oliver (Town)* 91n46, 95n61, 135–37

Quebec (Attorney General) v. *Canada (National Energy Board)* [Hydro Quebec] 135–37

Quebec (Attorney General) v. *Moses* 46n76, 98n74, 135–37

R. v. *Badger* 24, 28, 32–33

R. v. *Gladstone* 93

Regina v. *George* 25, 31–32

R. v. *Lewis* 90n42, 118, 144n28

R. v. *Marshall [No. 1]* 24, 28, 32–34, 150

R. v. *Sparrow* 10, 24, 34–37, 52–53, 95, 102, 112
fiduciary-based vs. honour-based accountability in 13, 16, 36–37, 81–82, 87–89, 106–07,
general guiding principle 13, 35, 41, 75, 102, 106, 117
test for fiduciary accountability 39, 82, 89–90, 99, 110, 117, 130–32

R. v. *Sundown* 34

R. v. *Taylor and Williams* 22, 25, 35

R. v. *Van der Peet* 37, 43

Simon v. *The Queen* 34

Taku River Tlingit First Nation v. *British Columbia (Project Assessment Director)* 10n4, 37, 46n76

Tsilhqot'in Nation v. *British Columbia* 11, 121, 129, 130n13&14, 131, 140n25

Wewaykum Indian Band v. *Canada* 11, 14, 42n61, 66–67, 76, 83, 91, 150
test for fiduciary accountability 93, 96–98, 101, 121, 125, 126–30

HISTORIC CASES (pre to early 1900s)

Province of Ontario v. *Dominion of Canada and Province of Quebec; In re Indian Claims* 31

Ontario Mining Co. Ltd. v. *Seybold* 30

Province of Ontario v. *Dominion of Canada* 31

Doe d. Henderson v. *Westover* 29, 32

St. Catharines Milling and Lumber Co. v. *The Queen* 12n11

JAMIE D. DICKSON IS VICE-PRESIDENT IN CHARGE OF LEGAL AFFAIRS AT Des Nedhe Development, the economic development organization of English River First Nation in Saskatchewan. Prior to that, he worked in private practice with a national business law firm, as corporate counsel for a major resource development company, and as a consultant for First Nations in various contexts.

Dickson has represented both First Nations and industry in negotiating major collaboration agreements in the resources sector. Notably, Dickson has successfully negotiated multi-million-dollar agreements in both Saskatchewan and Western Australia. Having acted extensively for both First Nations and industry, Dickson brings a unique perspective to the issues examined in this book.

In 2014, Dickson completed his Master of Laws program at the University of Saskatchewan. As part of that program, he wrote a master's thesis entitled "The Honour of the Crown: Making Sense of Crown Liability Doctrine in Crown/Aboriginal Law in Canada." That thesis formed the basis for this book.

Dickson lives in Saskatoon with his wife Anna and son Calvin.